Readings in Literary Criticism 13

CRITICS ON WHITMAN

Readings in Literary Criticism

CRITICS ON
WHITMAN

Readings in Literary Criticism
Edited by Richard H. Rupp

University of Miami Press
Coral Gables, Florida

CONTENTS

ACKNOWLEDGMENTS

Richard P. Adams: from *PMLA*, vol. 72, 1957. Copyright © 1957 by the Modern Language Association of America. Reprinted by permission of the publisher.

Gay Wilson Allen: from *Walt Whitman As Man, Poet, and Legend*. Copyright © 1961 by Southern Illinois University Press. Reprinted by permission of the publisher.

Roger Asselineau: from *The Evolution of Walt Whitman: The Creation of A Book*. Copyright © 1962 by the President and Fellows of Harvard College. Reprinted by permission of the Belknap Press of Harvard University Press.

V. K. Chari: from "Structure and Poetic Growth in *Leaves of Grass*," *Walt Whitman Review*, vol. 9, 1963. Copyright © 1963 by Wayne State University Press. Reprinted by permission of the publisher.

Richard Chase: from *Walt Whitman Reconsidered*. Copyright © 1955 by Richard Chase. Reprinted by permission of William Morrow and Company, Inc.

Charles Feidelson, Jr.: from *Symbolism and American Literature*. Copyright © 1953 by The University of Chicago. Reprinted by permission of the publisher.

Martin Green: from *Re-Appraisals: Some Common Sense Readings in American Literature*. Copyright © 1965, 1963 by Martin Green. Reprinted by permission of W. W. Norton Company, Inc.

Randall Jarrell: from *Poetry and the Age*. Copyright © 1952, 1953 by Randall Jarrell. Reprinted by permission of Alfred A. Knopf, Inc.

D. H. Lawrence: from *Studies in Classic American Literature*. Copyright 1923, renewed 1951 by Frieda Lawrence. Reprinted by permission of The Viking Press, Inc.

R. W. B. Lewis: from *The American Adam: Innocence, Tragedy, and Tradition in the Nineteenth Century*. Copyright © 1955 by The University of Chicago. Reprinted by permission of the publisher.

Louis L. Martz: from *The Poem of the Mind: Essays on Poetry/English and American*. Copyright © 1966, 1969 by Louis L. Martz. Reprinted by permission of Oxford University Press, Inc.

Sister Eva Mary: from "Shades of Darkness in 'The Sleeper,' " *Walt Whitman Review*, vol. 15, 1969. Copyright © 1969 by Wayne State University Press. Reprinted by permission of the publisher.

F. O. Matthiessen: from *American Renaissance*. Copyright © 1941 by Oxford University Press, Inc. Reprinted by permission of the publisher.

James E. Miller, Jr.: from *A Critical Guide to Leaves of Grass*. Copyright © 1957 by The University of Chicago Press. Reprinted by permission of the publisher.

John A. Nagle: from "Toward a Theory of Structure in 'Song of Myself,' " *Walt Whitman Review*, vol. 15, 1969. Copyright © 1969 by Wayne State University Press. Reprinted by permission of the publisher.

Roy Harvey Pearce: from *The Continuity of American Poetry*. Copyright © 1961 by Princeton University Press. Reprinted by permission of the publisher.

Ezra Pound: "A Pact" from *Personae*. Copyright 1926 by Ezra Pound. Reprinted by permission of New Directions Publishing Corporation.

Stephen E. Whicher: "Whitman's Awakening to Death," in *The Presence of Walt Whitman: Selected Papers from the English Institute*. Copyright © 1962 by Columbia University Press. Reprinted by permission of the publisher.

INTRODUCTION

A FRIEND of mine once served a tour of duty as a junior naval officer in Hong Kong. Shortly after his ship arrived he was invited to a party, where he was introduced to a young British naval officer at the bar. "You're an American?" My friend nodded. His British counterpart drew himself up to his full height and declared, "I simply cahn't stahnd Whitman." American: Whitman. To him the two were identical.

Are they? What does it mean to be an American? An answer is not so simple as it once seemed. The existence of an "American" character is an assumption vigorously questioned in our time. *Leaves of Grass* raises the question again by forcing us to measure our own responses to experience against those of Walt Whitman, American. Perhaps no other term of identity suits him so well. One reason for reading *Leaves of Grass* then is to seek the common idiom which binds an American poet to an American reader.

When we speak of a national experience in literary terms we are speaking of epic. And, as Randall Jarrell points out, Whitman is epic, like *Moby-Dick*. But epic in a special sense. Whitman presumes to be the national self. Experience is personal for him, nonhistorical, nonlinear. I am what I can feel, he tells us, and what I feel you shall feel. Together we are America; there is no other. Thus Whitman subsumes national history in personal experience. Again, in Jarrell's words, "WALT WHITMAN: HE HAD HIS NERVE." The poet circles and expands himself over the continent, embracing all, rejecting none. The point to remember is that this is idealized experience, the vital *as if* without which poetic connections are impossible. The real self is not his, not yours, not mine, but the plangent, abstract, unitary self. We see this clearly in "Song of Myself," a poem impersonal and didactic, a poem on how to be an American.

"Song of Myself" is the central poem and the prototype of all the rest. Here the poet transforms himself from differences, distinctions, and isolated particularity to a diffused, passive, imaginative sensibility. Unlike Emerson, Whitman did not intuit God or the Oversoul, but rather the otherness of other people. He set out to reconcile that otherness with his own experience. To name something other was to make it one's own and to bring all people into the central self. "Song of Myself" is a magnificent act of faith in the transcendent unity of human experience.

Moreover, the central poem sets up a poetic self through which we experience the rest of the book. That self is ubiquitous because it is coextensive with all readers, wherever they live. It invites the reader to join the huge party of one on its ramble down the open road. The self is eternal because it merges with the organic flow of life, ever dying, ever renewing itself: "I am the grass." Furthermore, the self is paradigmatic or exemplary in that it shows us how to feel, how to live. Finally, it is mystical because it attempts to transcend the limitations of time, place, and mortality to gaze on the face of God.

Perhaps Whitman's most significant insight was the newness of the American experience. He comes to us as Adam early in the morning, into his garden the world. Surely no other poet has made so much of his own innocence or, of the implicit goodness in all that is. For Whitman, as for Augustine, evil does not exist. Augustine saw evil as an absence in reality; Whitman did not see it at all—at first. Later, in poems like "I Sit and Look Out," he can only wonder in silence at the sorrows of the world. We can reject him for his naivety or we can try to see the naivety in a larger perspective. Was it not necessary for the kind of poetry he was writing?

Nor is naivety dead. Grass has a new meaning today; it is part of a life-style which we have forgotten was ours. Call it Dionysiac, vagabond, beat, hippie, or what you will, the passionate, unfettered cry for the simple goodness of life has echoed throughout our history. Whitman's grass, it is true, does not come to us rolled in cigarette papers, but it produces highs just the same. Whatever our misgivings about perverse and arrogant innocence in contemporary American life (in which rudeness is often mistaken for honesty), we ought not to neglect the exhiliration which Whitman's poetry can give us and the way in which that exhiliration helps us to understand the present.

This anthology of criticism is divided into five sections. The first section shows us the recognition granted Whitman by his fellow poets. Ezra Pound, surely the most un-Whitmanesque of poets, makes his peace with Whitman in "A Poet." Ralph Waldo Emerson recognizes his genius in the most important letter in American literature (never mind that Whitman's use of the letter to puff the second edition of *Leaves* miffed Emerson). Henry David Thoreau dislikes Whitman's sensuality but shows enthusiasm nonetheless.

Section two of the anthology gives us the design of the book.V. K. Chari classifies the individual poems in an effort to establish the poetic growth in *Leaves of Grass.* John Nagle uses structural analysis to discover eight phases of development in the central poem, "Song of Myself."

Section three presents four different approaches to Whitman's poetry. F. O. Matthiessen concentrates on diction and language in a selection from his classic study, *American Renaissance.* R. W. B. Lewis shows how Whitman, an American Adam, makes a new world out of his own experience. Randall Jarrell suggests that lines and whole passages need to be read to get the essential genius of Whitman—and he proceeds to point out the fauna of *Leaves* like an enthusiastic, peripatetic curator.

In section four some major poems are selected for close analysis. Richard Chase deals extensively with the poet's identity in "Song of Myself." Stephen E. Whicher shows Whitman's growing awareness of death as the central reality in "Out of the Cradle Endlessly Rocking." Charles Feidelson discusses the symbols in "When Lilacs Last in the Dooryard Bloom'd," while Richard P. Adams points out the significant uses (and omissions) of pastoral convention in that poem. Critic and scholar complement each other here. James E. Miller, Jr., sees the soul's return to God through space, time, and death in his reading of "Passage to India." In her analysis of "The Sleepers," Sister Eva Mary, O.S.F., relates the images of darkness to the theme of transcendent hope in the poem. Gay Wilson Allen, perhaps the dean of Whitman scholars today, treats several of Whitman's shorter poems.

The final section presents some conclusions. D. H. Lawrence, first of all, suggests some reservations about Whitman. Roy Harvey Pearce argues that Whitman's poetic self emerges primarily in opposition to its world—opposing himself directly to Lewis. Louis L. Martz relates Whitman's prophetic stance and tone to his reading of the Old Testament prophets. Martin Green, another Englishman, demythologizes Twain and Whitman together, contending that both are antiliterary. Roger Asselineau, convinced that Whitman's chief problem was homosexuality, concludes his fine two-volume study by insisting on the success of Whitman the poet at the expense of Whitman the man.

The titles for these selections are generally the critics' own, but I have supplied titles for the readings from Lewis, Weimer, Allen, Lawrence, and Pearce.

The bibliography is highly selective and concentrates on full-length studies rather than articles. My assumption is that the books are more readily accessible than the articles, and that they will stimulate further study of Whitman. Who knows? Perhaps reading will help to change the mind of that British naval officer in Hong Kong—and his American cousins.

University of Miami, 1971   RICHARD H. RUPP

TABLE OF IMPORTANT DATES

1819	Born May 31 at West Hills, Long Island.
1830-34	Apprentice printer.
1836-39	Teaches on Long Island.
1841-42	Lives in New York as writer and editor.
1846-48	Edits Brooklyn *Daily Eagle* ; February 1848, goes to New Orleans to work on the *Crescent* ; leaves for home May 27.
1848-49	Edits an abolitionist newspaper, the Brooklyn *Freeman*.
1850-54	Free lance writer, printer, builder, and real estate speculator.
1855	July, prints *Leaves of Grass;* Emerson writes to him July 21.
1856	2nd edition of *Leaves*.
1860	In Boston for 3rd edition of *Leaves*.
1862-63	In Fredericksburg and Washington.
1864	Ill; returns to Brooklyn June 22.
1865	Returns to Washington; in May, *Drum-Taps* printed.
1868	4th edition of *Leaves*, with *Drum-Taps and Sequel.*
1870	Depressed; 5th edition of *Leaves; Democratic Vistas, Passage to India* printed (dated 1871).
1873	January 23, suffers paralytic stroke; mother dies May 23; moves to Camden, New Jersey, with his brother George.
1875	Prepares Centennial Edition (6th) of *Leaves* and *Two Rivulets* (dated 1876).
1879	Goes west for the first time and visits Colorado; ill, he remains with his brother Jeff in St. Louis during the fall.
1882	7th-8th editions of *Leaves* marred by threats of suppression from District Attorney; *Specimen Days and Collect.*
1884	Buys a home on Mickle Street, Camden, New Jersey.
1887	Thomas Eakins paints his portrait.
1888	*November Boughs*.
1891	*Good-Bye My Fancy* printed; "deathbed edition" of *Leaves* (dated 1891-92).
1892	Dies March 26; buried in Harleigh Cemetery, Camden.

EZRA POUND

A Pact

I make a pact with you, Walt Whitman—
I have detested you long enough.
I come to you as a grown child
Who has had a pig-headed father;
I am old enough now to make friends.
It was you that broke the new wood,
Now is a time for carving.
We have one sap and one root—
Let there be commerce between us.

From *Selected Poems of Ezra Pound* (New York: New Directions, 1956), p. 27.

RALPH WALDO EMERSON

Letter to Whitman: July 21, 1855

DEAR SIR—I am not blind to the worth of the wonderful gift of *Leaves of Grass*. I find it the most extraordinary piece of wit and wisdom that America has yet contributed. I am very happy in reading it, as great power makes us happy. It meets the demand I am always making of what seemed the sterile and stingy Nature, as if too much handiwork, or too much lymph in the temperament, were making our Western wits fat and mean.

I give you joy of your free and brave thought. I have great joy in it. I find comparable things said incomparably well, as they must be. I find the courage of treatment which so delights us, and which large perception only can inspire.

I greet you at the beginning of a great career, which yet must have had a long foreground somewhere, for such a start. I rubbed my eyes a little, to see if this sunbeam were no illusion; but the solid sense of the book is a sober certainty. It has the best merits, namely, of fortifying and encouraging.

I did not know until I last night saw the book advertised in a newspaper that I could trust the name as real and available for a post-office. I wish to see my benefactor, and have felt much like striking my tasks and visiting New York to pay you my respects.

R. W. EMERSON

From *Literature in America,* ed. Philip Rahv (New York: Meridian Books, 1957), p. 147.

HENRY DAVID THOREAU

Concerning Walt Whitman: December 7, 1856 (A Letter to Harrison Blake)

THAT WALT WHITMAN, of whom I wrote to you, is the most interesting fact to me at present. I have read his second edition (which he gave me), and it has done me more good than any reading for a long time. Perhaps I remember best the poem of Walt Whitman, an American, and the Sun-Down Poem. There are two or three pieces in the book which are disagreeable to say the least; simply sensual. He does not celebrate love at all. It is as if the beasts spoke. I think that men have not been ashamed of themselves without reason. No doubt there have always been dens where such deeds were unblushingly recited, and it is no merit to compete with their inhabitants. But even on this side he has spoken more truth than any American or modern that I know. I have found his poem exhilarating, encouraging. As for its sensuality—and it may turn out to be less sensual than it appears—I do not so much wish that those parts were not written, as that men and women were so pure that they could read them without harm, that is, without understanding them. One woman told me that no woman could read it—as if a man could read what a woman could not. Of course Walt Whitman can communicate to us no experience, and if we are shocked, whose experience is it that we are reminded of?

On the whole, it sounds to me very brave and American, after whatever deductions. I do not believe that all the sermons, so called, that have been preached in this land put together are equal to it for preaching.

We ought to rejoice greatly in him. He occasionally suggests something a little more than human. You can't confound him with the other inhabitants of Brooklyn or New York. How they must shudder when they read him! He is awfully good.

To be sure I sometimes feel a little imposed on. By his heartiness and broad generalities he puts me in a liberal frame of mind prepared to see wonders—as it were, sets me upon a hill or in the midst of a plains—stirs me well up, and then—throws in a thousand of brick. Though rude and sometimes ineffectual, it is a great primitive poem—an alarm or trumpet-note ringing through the American camp. Wonderfully like the Orientals, too, considering that when I asked him if he had read them, he answered, "No: tell me about them." . . .

Since I have seen him, I find that I am not disturbed by any brag or egoism in his book. He may turn out the least of a braggart of all, having a better right to be confident.

He is a great fellow.

From *Literature in America,* ed. Philip Rahv (New York: Meridian Books, 1957), pp. 148-49.

V. K. CHARI

Structure and Poetic Growth in *Leaves of Grass*

WHITMAN SHAPED the structure of *Leaves of Grass* through a lifetime of labor and insisted that the book was a 'unity.' He personally supervised the 'Death-Bed' Edition and recommended it as his final arrangement of the poems. He even placed an injunction on future editors not to tamper with the order of the poems. This has naturally led critics to believe that there is a structure to the volume that is inviolable, though there has been no agreement as to the specific nature of that structure.

Explorations of the structural pattern of the *Leaves of Grass* have been attempted by William Sloane Kennedy, Irving Story and James E. Miller, Jr. These analyses are very useful in that they try to explain the selection and ordering of the poems into various interrelated groups. Kennedy's grouping is based upon subject-matter and arranges the poems into three major divisions: 1.) Poems of Life and Body, 2.) Poems of Democracy, and 3.) Poems of Religion. Kennedy claimed that his classification accorded with Whitman's objects announced in the 1876 Preface. But I think that such divisions are manifestly false. For the whole of Whitman's poetry proceeds from a central unity of experience and expresses an integrated vision so as not to permit an artificial division of its themes into those of self, of democracy, of religion and so on (they are so interfused). For example, it is difficult to see how 'Brooklyn Ferry' is a poem of 'life and body' purely and 'Prayer of Columbus' a poem of religion, unless we interpret 'religion' in the sense of conventional faith; but Whitman, in the best part of his poetry, never understood religion that way.

A proper appreciation of this basic unity of theme in Whitman's poetry is shown by Professor Miller. According to Miller, Whitman arranged his poems not strictly in accordance with the subject-matter, but in accordance with the 'shifting focus of the pervading theme.' Thus in the basic three-part structure that he discovers in the book there is, first, the creation of the Prototype of the New World Personality (the Self), secondly, its engagement with *'the time and land we swim in,'* the 19th century America, and finally, its preoccupation with the 'spiritual law.' Professor Miller, thus, notices that in the last group of poems the focus shifts to the domain of spirituality. This theme of spirituality, not new in the book by any means, becomes of central importance in the group of poems in which are included 'Proud Music,' 'Passage to India,' 'Columbus,' 'Sleepers,' 'To Think of Time,' and 'Whispers of Heavenly Death.' Miller's most valuable point is that the whole of *Leaves of Grass* is centered round the theme of the Self, and this is clearly in accordance with Whitman's own intention. In a sense, the whole of Whitman's poetry deals with the Self's engagement with itself and the world around, with time and space. The sense of the Self's engagement is never absent in Whitman. This applies even to his War Poems, and even poems expressing an emotional crisis like some 'Calamus' pieces and the Sea-Shore and Elegiac poems. However, I would here like to think, with Malcolm Cowley to some extent, that Whitman's vision of the Dynamic Self is best expressed in 'Song of Myself' and poems of that order (which include 'The Sleepers,' 'Brooklyn Ferry,' 'Salut Au Monde,' 'Paumonok,' the several 'Songs,' and 'Passage to India'), in what Whitman called songs of 'dilation and pride,' and that this vision was periodically blurred or weakened, though never completely lost, through the poet's career, and that in his old age poems it is further weakened and modified. Therefore, I would prefer to separate the poems in which the vision of the Self is most triumphant from the poems which are in a different tone, and those in which there is a decline in poetic vision and vigor. But Miller's analysis, committed as it is to a defence of the present structure, has to justify what seems to me an indiscriminate lumping together of poems of different orders and tones, and poems which are far apart both chronologically and stylistically. Such a defence explains neither chronology nor poetic growth, nor thematic arrangement, if the poems are read with close understanding.

But Miller's analysis has the advantage that it seeks to discover the poet's scheme, for there is no doubt that Whitman worked out a deliberate scheme, and this is essentially a sound critical approach. To support Professor Miller's thesis of the 'shifting focus' in the book we have Whitman's own declared intention that 'after chanting in Leaves of Grass the songs of the body and existence, to then compose a further . . . volume' making 'the unseen soul govern absolutely at last.' Kennedy, Miller and Stovall ('Main Drifts') bank on this statement. But my own fear is that the statement is misleading. Whatever Whitman's intention may have been, I am not prepared to believe that 'Song of Myself' is any whit less spiritual than, say, 'Prayer of Columbus.' On the other hand, I am persuaded that in the 'Columbus' poem there is a marked weakening of the poet's pristine vision of the Self, and poetically too, it is a very much weakened utterance, being pathetic in tone, and in spite of its unity and dramatic form achieves neither the symbolic richness nor the deep elegiac tone of 'Lilacs' or 'Out of the Cradle.' Therefore, to say that in 'Song of Myself' Whitman celebrated the body or physical existence and that in 'Columbus' he staged a 'free entry into the spiritual world' would be a travesty, for it would miss the whole point of Whitman's mysticism.

Another objection I have to this grouping is that it does not explain how a poem like 'The Sleeper,' originally of the First Edition, which is in Whitman's earliest mode and resembles 'Song of Myself' in both subject-matter and style, may be grouped with 'Columbus' and other old-age poems. I wish further to ask how there is in the poem a shift in focus from 'Song of Myself.' I do not quite understand why Whitman himself planted the poem where it is now, instead of letting it remain with the 'Song of Myself' group where it belongs. The case of 'The Sleepers' is just one example. There are others which in their present positions seem clearly misplaced. It is rather difficult to discover the rationale for the present structure,[1] though undeniably some of the clusters like 'Inscriptions,' 'Children of Adam,' 'Calamus,' 'Drum-Taps,' and the clusters of old-age poems possess unity, both chronological and thematic; but even in them there are inconsistencies. A more satisfactory ordering would have been one that is based 1.) either on chronology, 2.) on the difference in the modes of expression, or 3.) on subject-matter. But Whitman, as is well known, deliberately developed a structure that is not chronological. But chronology is very important for the study of Whitman's poetry.

Exploration of the structure of *Leaves of Grass* involves evaluation and grading of the poems in terms of poetic growth; it even brings up problems of interpretation. As regards this, there have been two opposite views; one, that Whitman had attained his fullest poetic stature in the First Edition and did not register any significant advance after that, he even went down, and the other that he did develop both in his vision and his art from a less to a more mature state. A final settlement of this issue is perhaps impossible, but its shape will be determined by whether one chooses a poem like 'Song of Myself ' as one's model of perfection or 'Lilacs.' The values by which one makes one's choice will always vary. But perhaps there is no need to make this kind of exclusive choice so far as Whitman's poetry is concerned.

In this connection, a most valuable idea for Whitman criticism is Professor Gay Wilson Allen's theory of 'mutations in Whitman's art.'[2] That Whitman changed from one mode to another and wrote in three distinct styles, Allen has shown; and though perhaps this was known before, its importance for our appreciation of Whitman has been rightly emphasized by Allen. So far, evaluations of Whitman have swung between the two extremes of Eliot's exclusive admiration of the elegiac poems and Malcolm Cowley's unqualified enthusiasm for 'Song of Myself,' which leads him to think that Whitman wrote nothing worthwhile after the First Edition and that his poetic vision declined after that. It is, therefore, important to recognize, as Allen insists, that Whitman wrote poems which are 'good in different ways'[3] and that there need not necessarily be a choice 'between' 'Song of Myself ' and 'Lilacs.' I accept this position with one reservation. While the Sea-Shore lyrics and the Lincoln Elegy are certainly great poems, and while some of the 'short' poems too like 'Noiseless Patient Spider' and 'Dalliance of the Eagles' achieve a compactness and finish that is not in the 'Song of Myself,' I think that any total estimate of Whitman's poetic achievement has to be based on 'Song of Myself ' and poems of that order. They are Walt Whitman's unique contribution to world literature. They possess freshness and originality, boldness of vision and power of utterance that is all

1. See De Selincourt's view that the poems as finally arranged by Whitman fail to be 'comprehensible' as a unity 'not merely in the sense that they explain but rather in the sense that they fulfill one another.' Quoted by Sholom J. Kahn, *Walt Whitman Review*, V (June 1959), 25.

2. *Walt Whitman as Man, Poet, and Legend* (Carbondale: Southern Illinois University Press, 1961), pp. 46-62.

3. See his review of Malcolm Cowley's edition of *Leaves of Grass* (1855), *New York Times Book Review*, 28 February 1960, p. 42.

	I	II	III	IV	Remarks
	'Songs' of 'Dilation and Pride'	Poems of emotional crisis & Elegiac Poems	Drum-Taps & Patriotic Poems	'Old-Age Echoes'	
MODE I	1855: First Edition Poems 1856: 'Salut au Monde,' 'Songs' of 'Open Road,' etc. 'Brooklyn Ferry,' 'Spontaneous Me' 1860: 'Paumonok,' 'Song of Joys,' 'Old Feuillage,' 'Scented Herbage,' 'Song at Sun-Set,' 'From Pent-Up Aching Rivers,' 'One Hour to Madness and Joy,' 'In Paths Untrodden,' 'Me Imperturbe,' 'I Hear America Singing' 1865: 'Rise O Days from Your Fathomless Deeps,' 'Give Me the Splendid Silent Sun,' 'To the Leaven'd Soil They Trod' ('Drum-Taps') 1868: 'Proud Music of the Storm' 1870: 'Warble for Lilac Time' 1871: 'Song of the Exposition' 1872: 'Mother With Thy Equal Blood' 'Mystic Trumpeter'	'Of the Terrible Doubt,' etc. ('Calamus')		'You Tides with Ceaseless Swell' (1888) 'On, On the Same, Ye Jocund Twain' (1891) { 'The Unexpress'd' (1891) 'Grand is the Seen' 'Unseen Buds' (1891)	*Shorter poems: both in style and tone akin to 'Song of Myself.'
MODE II	1865: 'Pioneers! O Pioneers!' 1868: 'Passage to India' 1876: 'Eidolons'	'Out of the Cradle' (1859) 'As I Ebb'd' (1860) 'Lilacs' (1865) 'Columbus' (1874) 'With Husky Haughty Lips' (1884)	'First O Song for a Prelude' ('Drum-Taps')		**Turgrid, doctrinaire, but stylistically in the early mode.
MODE III	1871: 'Sparkles from the Wheel' 1876: 'Locomotive in Winter' 1874: 'After the Sea-Ship' 1880: 'Patrolling Barnegat' 'Dalliance of the Eagles' 1867: 'One's-Self I Sing' 1874: 'Come Said My Soul'		'Beat! Beat! Drums' (1861) 'Song of the Banner' (1861) 'By the Bivouac's Fitful Flame' (1865) 'The Wound-Dresser' (1865) 'Cavalry Crossing a Ford' (1865)	'Sail Out for Good Eidolon Yacht' (1891) 'Halcyon Days' (1891) 'Short Pieces' *	*Short pieces: mostly weakened in tone; to be read as annexes to the central *L. of G.*; reviews of themes; 'the surplusage or the wake eddying behind it?' (Whitman). **Also cryptic poems (e.g. 'Inscription') spread over the *Leaves*

Whitman's own. In this category I would include all the expansive poems or 'Songs'; and also 'Brooklyn Ferry' and 'The Sleepers,' which have the unique distinction of being at once unified poems with richness of symbol and development, and expansive poems in the 'Song of Myself' mode. Mr Cowley will support me in expressing this preference (which is but a preference) to 'Song of Myself.' Both Cowley and myself set much store by Whitman's conception of 'Selfhood,' which finds its most glorious expression in the poems listed above, and this predilection determines our approach to Whitman's poetry. Here, however, I do not go entirely with Cowley in saying that after 1855 Whitman's mystical vision declined. I hold that Whitman wrote several very good 'expansive' poems after 1855, 'A Song of Joys' and 'Passage to India,' to name but two. I do not also share Cowley's rejection of the 'Lilacs' as an inferior piece.

Though undeniably, as Professor Allen has pointed out, Whitman wrote in different modes, it is perhaps difficult to argue that he strictly developed from one mode to another. For instance, it can be shown that Whitman continued writing in his early (1855) style until well on to 1868 or 1871. In fact, Whitman did not till the very end abandon the catalogue style. The 1860 Edition which contained many short lyrics also contained long poems, some of them major poems, like 'Starting from Paumonok,' 'A Song of Joys,' 'Our Old Feuillage,' which, despite their unequal quality, are still very much like 'Song of Myself.' Moreover, even some of the shorter pieces like 'In Paths Untrodden' ('Calamus') and 'Me Imperturbe' ('Inscriptions') are comparable to individual sections of 'Song of Myself,' which, too, often achieve this kind of unity. But 'Out of the Cradle' and 'Lilacs,' which, according to Allen, are in Whitman's middle style, are quite different, of course, as not only do they approximate to a musical structure, they employ 'dramatic voices' as a technical device, and poems like 'Sparkles from the Wheel,' 'Noiseless Patient Spider' or 'Dalliance of the Eagles' are best examples of Whitman's accomplishment in the third mode, the compact form. 'Eidolons' and 'O Pioneers' have verse structures that are nearly regular. But as I have pointed out, Whitman wrote these kinds of poems during periods in which he also wrote other kinds. I, therefore, attempt in the following Table an 'inclusive' grouping of Whitman's major poems, based on considerations of poetic growth, difference in poetic modes, as shown by Allen, unity of tone and image, and thematic arrangement. I do not, of course, make so bold as to suggest a re-edition of Leaves of Grass; [4] but I believe that a grouping on the following lines may prove useful to an understanding of Whitman's poems.

From "Structure and Poetic Growth in Leaves of Grass," Walt Whitman Review, 9 (1963), 58-63.

---

4. See Sholom J. Kahn: 'Towards a Popular Edition of Whitman's "Complete Poems," ' Walt Whitman Review, V (June 1959), 23-26.

JOHN M. NAGLE

Toward a Theory of Structure in *"Song of Myself"*

'SONG OF MYSELF,' the longest poem in Walt Whitman's collection of poems *Leaves of Grass*, presents any reader with a considerable challenge. The poem consists of a total of 1346 lines of poetry, and though Whitman has divided those 1346 lines into 52 'sections' or 'paragraphs' or 'chants,' their marked variations in length and scope tend to add to the puzzle that is the poem rather than help to clarify it. The shortest of these sections is six lines long while the longest contains more than 150 lines. The scope of ideas treated throughout the poem is practically impossible to describe, for there is little either within or beyond the universe that does not at some point come under the close scrutiny of the poet. Body, soul, life, death, earth, sea, time, space, God, man—all, and more too, are dealt with by Whitman at various times and to various degrees throughout the 1346 lines. The poem ranges in tone from the almost ecstatic and graphic account of the sexual union of body and soul to the narrative summary of a futile and disastrous sea battle, from the dispassionate listing of a multitude of sense impressions to the exultant and triumphant experiencing of the Unknown.

It is little wonder then that a first reading of 'Song of Myself' leaves the uninitiated Whitman student gasping for breath and explanation, frustrated by what he knows he has missed and exhausted by what he thinks he has understood. After several subsequent readings, however, this same student may begin to see some interrelationships within the total poem and he may very well ask the following question: 'Did Walt Whitman deliberately structure his poem, or is it really the amorphous mass of fleeting sense impressions and inexplicable abstractions that it seemed to be after my first reading?' It is this exact question, 'Is there deliberate structure in "Song of Myself"?' and its expansion, 'If so, what *is* the structure and how does Whitman maintain it?' that will provide focus for the discussion which follows.

Several hypotheses will guide that discussion's development: first, that Whitman's 'Song of Myself' is a carefully structured poem, made up of distinguishable parts or phases joined to form a unified whole (as used in the remainder of this discussion, the term 'section' will refer to one of Whitman's fifty-two divisions; the term 'phase' will refer to the grouping of several sections); second, that Whitman's repetition of themes and symbols and his clear transitional signals enable the reader to follow the poem's movement from section to section and phase to phase; and third, that each section, including the so-called 'catalogues,' has a definite structure and movement. Without attempting to view the poem as anything but what it is, a sensitive reader should be aware of Whitman's conscious structure and organization. To get at these more precisely, I should like to look first at the structure of a single phase, then to apply the same sort of analysis to the total poem, and finally to move back again to examination of several other parts of the poem which reflect Whitman's conscious effort to structure the 1346 lines of 'Song of Myself.'

There is undoubtedly no more meaningful place to start in an analysis of a single phase of the poem than to look carefully at Sections 1-5, for these sections not only introduce many of the themes and ideas that pervade the rest of the poem, but they also illustrate nicely Whitman's concern for organization and his careful use of transitions. Basically, this first phase provides the focus for the rest of the poem. For instance, within the first five lines of the poem, Whitman focuses attention upon 'I' the poet, 'you' the reader, the inter-existence of all men, the material atom and body, the soul, and the 'spear of summer grass,' that all-important and unifying symbol in the poem. To indicate further its focusing characteristics, a list of other themes introduced in these first five sections will perhaps suffice:

—the evolutionary nature of the Self
—infinity of all, including time, heaven, hell, perfection
—the dialectic of life
—'creeds and schools in abeyance'
—'nature without check with original energy'
—an acceptance of all, good and bad
—the union of the Self with nature
—the Self's ability to interpenetrate all
—the everpresent 'procreant urge' of the world
—the perfect fitness and equanimity of all things
—the 'Me myself' apart from 'the pulling and hauling'
—the essential and beautiful union of body and soul
—love, 'a kelson of the creation'
—and the omnivorous nature of the poet

How often the remainder of the poem echoes these themes!

In terms of organization, Sections 1-5 are a unified whole, having conflict, climax and fulfillment. Sections 1-4 represent a reaching out, a grappling by the poet; Section 5 climaxes this search and concludes with the poet's undeniable assertions of what he knows to be true. The basic conflict between 'creeds and schools' and 'nature without check with original energy' is clearly presented in the first section of the phase and then is continually kept in view as the poet moves toward his climax in Section 5. In Section 2, for instance, Whitman contrasts the 'houses and rooms' which are full of perfumes to the 'atmosphere' which is not and the ability to read and 'get at the meaning of poems' to the possession of 'the origin of all poems.' In Section 3, this conflict is represented on one side by the 'talkers' who 'talk of the beginning and the end' and on the other by Whitman who talks not of beginning and end but of now as the time of greatest fulfillment. In Section 4, the 'talkers' become 'the trippers and askers' and in contrast to their 'pulling and hauling stands what I am,' the poet's 'Me myself.' Finally, after that climactic physical union of body and soul in Section 5, the poet brings out the conflict once more when he speaks of 'the peace and knowledge that pass all the argument of the earth.'

To recapitulate, on one side can be grouped the 'creeds and schools,' 'houses and rooms,' reckoning, reading and getting at poems, talkers talking, 'trippers and askers,' 'pulling and hauling,' and 'the argument of the earth'; on the other side, one can easily group 'nature without check with original energy,' 'the atmosphere,' 'the origin of all poems,' the completeness of 'now,' 'this mystery,' 'the perfect fitness and equanimity of things,' 'Me myself,' and 'peace and knowledge.' The climax of this conflict, that physical union of body and soul, enables the 'I' to assert with complete conviction his place in relation to the world around him. These assertions that end Section 5 are so all-inclusive and so sharply fixed that they automatically signal conclusion not only for Section 5 but for the total movement of this first phase.

In addition to his use of the organizational pattern of conflict-climax-fulfillment and his numerous illustrations of that conflict, Whitman maintains unity in the first phase by use of careful transitions within and between sections. This can be seen by once again tracing Whitman's development. Section 1 ends with the stated conflict between 'creeds and schools' and 'nature without check.' Section 2 is spaced by Whitman into five parts. In the first and fourth, he amplifies on 'creeds and schools'; in the second and fifth, he amplifies on 'nature without check'; in the third, he enumerates with images that appeal to the senses of touch, sight, smell, and sound exactly what he means by his madness to be undisguised, naked and in contact with the atmosphere. Section 3 begins with another example of the basic conflict, this time focusing on 'talkers.' Contrasting himself to these 'talkers,' the poet launches into a discussion of the 'procreant urge,' the dialectic of life, and the unity and equality of all, and he concludes with the rhetorical question of whether or not he should postpone his 'acceptation and realization' of 'this mystery' and turn to the petty, limited concerns of life. Section 4 immediately enumerates some of those petty concerns. At the conclusion of this brief listing, the poet actively answers the question previously raised when he divorces the 'Me myself' from the enumerated items of 'pulling and hauling.' Section 4 ends with the poet witnessing and waiting, and Section 5 presents that for which the poet has waited, the sexual union of body and soul. That fulfillment has been the result is evident in those final assertions already mentioned that clearly and powerfully drive the first phase to a close.

Let us now broaden our view and look to the total poem, for here too can be found indications of Whitman's deliberate structure and form. Focusing almost completely upon the poem itself and its transitional signals, and looking for organizational signals similar to those evident in the poem's first five sections, we find that the fifty-two sections seem to divide themselves into some eight unified phases. The first phase, consisting of Section 1-5, has already been discussed at some length. It, in effect, introduces the major themes of the whole poem and successfully focuses attention upon the self, the soul and body, and the artificial and real. The second phase begins with the question 'What is the grass?' and switches the focus for the moment from the poet to the child and his query. Conjecturing some answers to that question, the poet talks in Section 7 of his oneness with all of life and death and commands at the end of Section 7 that the world 'undrape' itself. Sections 8-16 reflect the poet's 'undraping' of life and death and his interpenetration of all. Section 17 asserts the universality of all the poet has presented in the prior sections and concludes with this strong, declarative answer to the original question raised in Section 6 (note that emphasis naturally falls on the first word):

> This is the grass that grows wherever the land is and the water is,
> This is the common air that bathes the globe.

Carrying this theme of equality and universality into Section 18, the poet asserts that he sings of all and to all, victors and vanquished; and on that note, the second phase constructed totally within the framework of the question 'What is the grass?' draws to a close.

Some of this commonality, however, spills over into the first half of Section 19, at which point the poet asks the question 'Do you guess I have some intricate purpose?' and, with that question, he makes his transition to his next topic: Who is this 'I' who speaks so astonishingly and what is he about? In almost whispered tones, Whitman concludes Section 19 with a personal assurance and invitation:

> This hour I tell things in confidence,
> I might not tell everybody, but I will tell you.

The first of these 'things' told in confidence is introduced in the first lines of Section 20 with another series of questions:

> Who goes there? hankering, gross, mystical, nude;
> How is it I extract strength from the beef I eat?
> What is man anyhow? what am I? what are you?

From Sections 19-25, the poet attempts to find answers to these questions, to identify himself and his reason for being. In Section 20, he is sound, solid, deathless and august; in 21, he is the poet of body and soul; in 21 and 22, he is at one with the night, earth and sea; in 23, he is the poet of En Masse, accepter of all. Finally in Section 24, he is able to name himself and his identity in the climactic assertion to which he has been building:

> Walt Whitman, a kosmos, of Manhattan the son,
> Turbulent, fleshy, sensual, eating, drinking and breeding . . .

From this point until the end of Section 25, the poet asserts the nobility of the body, attaches to nature the physical characteristics of humans, and affirms his abilities to impart. The definition of Self, introduced with the question, 'Who goes there?' back in Section 20 has been at least partially achieved by the end of Section 25, the end of the third phase.

Whereas the poet imparted in Sections 24-25, the first line of Section 26 indicates that he will now receive, and, by means of this shift, he launches into the fourth phase.

> Now I will do nothing but listen,
> To accrue what I hear into this song, to let sounds contribute toward it.

As he *listens* now rather than *expresses*, he becomes aware by the end of Section 26 of 'the puzzle of puzzles,/ And that we call Being,' and for the next six sections he tries to resolve that puzzle. He undergoes an almost sexual climax and fulfillment with the sense of touch, he explores the relationship of the world to the self, and he discovers that because 'All truths wait in all things,'

> I find I incorporate gneiss, coal, long-threaded moss, fruits,
>   grains, esculent roots,
> And am stucco'd with quadrupeds and birds all over,
> And have distanced what is behind me for good reasons,
> But call any thing back again when I desire it.

Section 32 climaxes this fourth phase when the poet rides the 'gigantic beauty of a stallion,' whose 'well-built limbs tremble with pleasure,' for it is this stallion which best symbolizes the primitive innocence and being which the poet has sought; he has found at least a partial answer to the 'puzzle of puzzles.'

The poet's exultation over his new found knowledge is initially expressed in the first lines of Section 33,

> Space and Time! now I see it is true, what I guess'd at,
> What I guess'd when I loaf'd on the grass,
> What I guess'd while I lay alone in my bed,
> And again as I walk'd the beach under the paling stars of the morning,

and this jubilation carries him through the first half of this longest of sections in which he once again interpenetrates all, though this time with increased insight:

> My ties and ballasts leave me, my elbows rest in sea-gaps,
> I skirt sierras, my palms cover continents,
> I am afoot with my vision.

Somewhat imperceptibly, as the poet skirts afoot with his vision, the nature of the interpenetration changes. Instead of sense impressions that call forth joy and exultation, they begin to call forth misery and woe, and by the end of Section 33, the poet is heading into what James E. Miller, Jr calls 'the dark night of the Soul.' Sections 34-37 reflect this dark night superbly, and in the final lines of Section 37 the poet not only identifies with but actually is in quick succession a convict in jail, a mutineer handcuffed, a larcener, a cholera patient, and a beggar sitting shamefaced with hat projected.

Having arrived at the utter depths of despair and misery in the final lines of Section 37, the poet has no where to go but up, and he projects himself forth with this undeniable exclamation in the first lines of Section 38:

> Enough! enough! enough!
> Somehow I have been stunn'd. Stand back!
> Give me a little time beyond my cuff'd head, slumbers, dreams, gaping.
> I discover myself on the verge of a usual mistake.

Exactly what that usual mistake is becomes the topic of the sixth phase of the poem, Sections 38-43, as the poet talks of faith in love, faith in the primitive and innocent, and finally faith in 'what is untried and afterward.' Uniting himself with Christ and with 'the friendly and flowing savage,' this poet-Christ-savage becomes the 'I' who in Sections 38-43 enunciates his faith as 'the greatest of faiths and the least of faiths.' Whereas the questions asked earlier in the third phase of the poem were 'What is a man anyhow? what am I? what are you?' the questions now asked in this sixth phase become 'And what is reason? and what is love? and what is life?' Certainly the poet's definition of himself, his total involvement with both the joys and miseries of existence, and his awakening to the significance of an omnivorous faith all of which have occurred between the two sets of questions have contributed to the increased depth of his understanding. The poet concludes Section 43, the last in this sixth phase, with another unquestionable assertion, this time that his faith in 'what is untried and afterward' can never fail.

In Section 44, the poet clearly begins the next phase of the poem and even more clearly defines its subject:

> It is time to explain myself—let us stand up.
> What is known I strip away,
> I launch all men and women forward with me into the Unknown.

From here to Section 50, the poet launches us all forth into the Unknown, into that faith which is 'untried and afterward.' Temporal and spatial limitations disappear as all become involved in the perpetual journey to the Unknown, the inevitable meeting with the great Camerado. In Section 46, the poet involves the reader directly when he echoes the self-reliance theme of the Transcendentalists:

> Not I, not any one else can travel that road for you,
> You must travel it for yourself . . .

You are also asking me questions and I hear you,
I answer that I cannot answer, you must find out for yourself.

As the poem moves toward its conclusion, the poet reaffirms the power of the
self over all—God, body, soul, death, life—when he writes that 'nothing, not
God, is greater to one than one's self is.' This seventh phase, the journey to
the Unknown, ends with a final three-line assertion:

I ascend from the moon, I ascend from the night,
I perceive that the ghastly glimmer is noonday sunbeams reflected,
And debouch to the steady and central from the offspring great or small.

In contrast to the strength of assertion and absoluteness in the last lines of
Section 49, nearly all of Section 50 seems tentative and hesitant. These last three
sections represent the final phase of the poem as the poet, exhausted but
satisfied, attempts to conclude his lines without concluding their movement.
Section 50 appears to be a halting effort to explain what has happened in the
preceding sections, but it ends unsuccessfully in an almost 'I give up' explosion
of explanations:

It is not chaos or death—it is form, union, plan—it is eternal life—
it is Happiness.

By Section 52, the poet, now less hesitant, has come to associate himself with
the spotted hawk, for neither is tame or translatable. All of which substantiates
what the poet has already affirmed, that 'Not I, not any one else can travel
that road for you.' Though the last lines focus on 'you' and though the identity
of the poet dissolves, the movement of the poem continues ever onward and
upward:

You will hardly know who I am or what I mean,
But I shall be good health to you nevertheless,
And filter and fibre your blood.

Failing to fetch me at first keep encouraged,
Missing me one place search another,
I stop somewhere waiting for you.

To review very, very briefly this organizational scheme based nearly solely
upon Whitman's transitional signals:

Phase I   (1-5):Focus upon the self, the grass, the body and soul;
                    introduction of recurrent themes in the poem.

Phase II   (6-18):The poet's initial penetration of the world out

there as he attempts to answer the question, 'What
is the grass?'

Phase III   (19-25):Identification of the poet, beginning of those things
to be told in confidence.

Phase IV   (26-32):The poet's attempt to solve the 'puzzle of puzzles'
by listening carefully to the 'sounds' of the world.

Phase V   (33-37):The 'puzzle" solved, Being revealed; the poet
actively participating in all, good and bad, joyful
and distressing.

Phase VI   (38-43):The importance of faith, the power of the poet-
Christ-savage, the 'untried and afterward.'

Phase VII (44-49):Flight to the Unknown.

Phase VIII (50-52):The poet exhausted but satisfied, stopping 'somewhere waiting for you.'

Certainly the earlier discussion of the first five sections of 'Song of Myself'
and the structural analysis just presented indicated definite attempts by Whitman to organize carefully the total poem. Attention should be given to several
additional structural techniques. Foremost among these is the poet's repetition
of significant themes and symbols—in much the same way that he handled
'creeds and schools' and 'nature without check with original energy' in the first
five sections. The relationships between body and soul and between life and
death exemplify two of the many recurrent themes in the poem. The grass,
probably the poem's central and outstanding symbol, is mentioned at least
seven times. In Section 1, the poet leans and loafes at his ease 'observing a spear
of summer grass,' and in Section 5 he asks the soul to join him while he loafes
on the grass; in Section 6, the poet asks the question 'What is the grass?' and
eleven sections later, he asserts, 'This is the grass that grows . . . '; in Section
31, he remarks that 'a leaf of grass is no less than the journey-work of the stars,'
and in Section 33 he exults that what he had guessed earlier when he loafed
on the grass is actually true; and in the final section, the poet again returns
to the grass when he writes, 'I bequeath myself to the dirt to grow from the
grass I love.'
    Whitman's organization of individual sections also contributes to the total
unity of the poem. Eight of the sections are introduced by questions, and, in
nearly every case, the poet attempts to answer in either that section or following
sections the questions which he has raised. Nearly fifteen of the sections begin
with clear-cut assertions about the self's identity, its beliefs or its knowledge,
and Whitman then goes on in the same section to illustrate or expand that
assertion. Examples of such assertions might include, 'I am the poet of the Body

and I am the poet of the Soul' (Section 21); 'All truths wait in all things' (Section 30); or 'I know I have the best of time and space, and was never measured and never will be measured' (Section 46). Sometimes the poet will discuss in two back-to-back sections two contrasting subjects. For instance, in Section 25, he focuses on speaking and writing, means of *expression;* in the next section, he shifts the focus to listening and absorption, means of *impression.* Or in Section 8, the poet focuses on urban images; in 9, on rural images. Often Whitman will suggest a topic in the last lines of one section and will amplify on that subject at length in the next section. For instance, in the last line of Section 6, he suggests the luck of dying, and then he deals directly with it in 7; in Section 27, he mentions the sense of touch and then focuses on it exclusively in 28-29.

One of Whitman's unique transitions occurs between Sections 24 and 25. At the end of 24, he focuses on a morning-glory, on daybreak, and on the erotic urge of the sunrise. His first line of Section 25 focuses on this same sunrise, but then in the second line, the poet changes the meaning of sunrise and it becomes something which goes out of himself; by the fifth line he has defined that sunrise going out of himself as his voice and the twirl of his tongue. In effect, it would seem that Whitman successfully turns the subject of one section (the sunrise) into a metaphor for the subject of the next section (his voice). Here are the lines that do it (Section 25):

> Dazzling and tremendous how quick the sun-rise would kill me,
> If I could not now and always send sun-rise out of me.
>
> We also ascend dazzling and tremendous as the sun,
> We found our own O my soul in the calm and cool of the daybreak.
>
> My voice goes after what my eyes cannot reach,
> With the twirl of my tongue I encompass worlds and volumes of worlds.

Finally, let's look briefly at Whitman's so-called 'catalogues.' These comprise a topic in themselves and what follows can hardly do justice to them; however, selected observations about the three longest 'catalogues,' Sections 15, 16 and 33, would seem to indicate a deliberate ordering or disordering on the part of Whitman. The first of these enumerates particular people, all of whom are doing something in the present tense. There is no obvious connection between any of them; in fact, they seem almost to be deliberately disordered. Several juxtapositions are most interesting: the duck shooter hunts and the deacons are ordained; the newly-come immigrants cover the wharf and the wooly-pates hoe in the sugar-field; the bride unrumples her white dress and the opium-eater reclines; the prostitute draggles her shawl and the president holds a cabinet meeting. As for the poet, he is simply a detached observer who does not appear until the final three lines:

> And these tend inward to me, and I tend outward to them,

And such as it is to be of these more or less I am,
And of these one and all I weave the song of myself.

Throughout the entire section, there is a slight hint that a calendar year is
passing, for we move from the children riding to a Thanksgiving dinner to a
First-day loafe to the hoeing of a sugar-field to a band concert to the Fourth
of July to a pike-fisher fishing through the ice. There is, however, a more
definite indication that night has come by the end of the section. It would
almost seem as if Whitman has superimposed a yearly cycle upon a daily one.

The second of these three 'catalogues,' Section 16 of the poem, is introduced
by the word 'I' and thereby focuses attention on the poet rather than on others.
This time the poet is less the detached observer and more the involved and
transcendent participant. This time, groups of people rather than individuals
are named, and these groups seem organized into contrasting pairs: the old and
young, the Southerner and the Northerner, the learner and the teacher. As the
poet clearly indicates in the first and last lines of the section . . . he now is
simultaneously a part of all of them. If time governs somewhat the organizational pattern in Section 15, then space serves a similar function in 16.

The final 'catalogue,' Section 33, consists of over 150 lines and comes during
that moment of ecstatic revelation when the poet feels he has solved the 'puzzle
of puzzles.' Somewhat ironically addressed to Space and Time, the lines defy
these, emphasizing that the poet is no longer limited by anything—time, space,
body, soul, sex. Rather, he is now able to interpenetrate all, not as a dispassionate observer of individuals or as an omnivorous part of groups, but as the people
themselves, able to assume their activities and places. The focus of this section,
therefore, is totally upon the poet and upon what he himself is doing. There
is no chronological or spatial ordering of items now, for time and space are
limitless. Rather, the items can be divided into those in the first half which
inspire rejoicing and those in the second half which inspire distress. Whereas
the first lines relate back to the 'common air that bathes the globe' and to the
poet's incorporation of all, the last lines lead nicely into the murder in cold
blood and the disastrous sea battle portrayed so dramatically in Sections 34-36.
If in fact there is definite structure and organization in these three sections,
it hardly seems valid to label them loosely as 'catalogues.'

The original questions raised for discussion were, 'Is there deliberate structure in "Song of Myself"?' and its expansion, 'If so, what is that structure and
how does Whitman maintain it?' The preceding discussion ought to suggest
some definite answers to those questions—answers which seem to move pro-
gressively forward toward a theory of structure in 'Song of Myself.'

From "Toward A Theory of Structure in 'Song of Myself,' " *Walt Whitman Review*, 15 (1969), 162-171.

Approaches to Whitman

F. O. MATTHIESSEN

Only A Language Experiment

NO ARRANGEMENT or rearrangement of Whitman's thoughts . . . can resolve the paradoxes or discover in them a fully coherent pattern. He was incapable of sustained logic, but that should not blind the reader into impatient rejection of the ebb and flow of his antitheses. They possess a loose dialectic of their own, and a clue of how to find it is provided by Engels' discussion of Feuerbach: 'One knows that these antitheses have only a relative validity; that that which is recognized now as true has also its latent false side which will later manifest itself, just as that which is now regarded as false has also its true side by virtue of which it could previously have been regarded as true.' Whitman's ability to make a synthesis in his poems of the contrasting elements that he calls body and soul may serve as a measure of his stature as a poet. When his words adhere to concrete experience and yet are bathed in imagination, his statements become broadly representative of humanity:

> I am she who adorn'd herself and folded her hair expectantly,
> My truant lover has come, and it is dark.

When he fails to make that synthesis, his language can break into the extremes noted by Emerson when he called it 'a remarkable mixture of the *Bhagvat-Geeta* and the *New York Herald.*' The incongruous lengths to which Whitman was frequently carried in each direction shows how hard a task he undertook. On the one hand, his desire to grasp American facts could lead him beyond slang into the rawest jargon, the journalese of the day. On the other, his attempts to pass beyond the restrictions of language into the atmosphere it could suggest often produced only the barest formulas. His inordinate and grotesque failures in both directions throw into clearer light his rare successes, and the fusion upon which they depend.

The slang that he relished as providing more fun than 'the books of all "the American humorists"' was what he heard in the ordinary talk of 'a gang of laborers, rail-road men, miners, drivers, or boatmen,' in their tendency 'to approach a meaning not directly and squarely' but by the circuitous routes of lively fancy. This tendency expressed itself in their fondness for nicknames like Old Hickory, or Wolverines, or Suckers, or Buckeyes. Their inventiveness had sowed the frontier with many a Shirttail Bend and Toenail Lake. Current evasions of the literal transformed a horsecar conductor into a 'snatcher,' straight whisky into 'barefoot,' and codfish balls into 'sleeve buttons.' But even though Whitman held such slang to be the source of all that was poetical in human utterance, he was aware that its fermentation was often hasty and frothy, and, except for occasional friendly regional epithets like Hoosiers or Kanucks, he used it only sparingly in his poems. Indeed, in some notes during the period of the gestation of his first *Leaves,* he advised himself to use 'common idioms and phrases—Yankeeisms and vulgarisms—cant expressions, when very pat only.' In consequence, the diction of his poetry is seldom as unconventional as that in the advice he gave himself for an essay on contemporary writing: 'Bring in a sock-dolager on the Dickens-fawners.' He gave examples of 'fierce words' in the *Primer* —'skulk,' 'shyster,' 'doughface,' 'mean cuss,' 'backslider,' 'lickspittle'—and sometimes cut loose in the talk that Traubel reported. But only on the rare occasions when he felt scorn did he introduce into his poems any expressions as savagely untrammelled as

> This now is too lamentable a face for a man,
> Some abject louse asking leave to be, cringing for it,
> Some milk-nosed maggot blessing what lets it wrig to its hole.

By contrast his most characteristic colloquialisms are easy and relaxed, as when he said 'howdy' to Traubel and told him that he felt 'flirty' or 'hunkydory,' or fell into slang with no self-consciousness, but with the careless aplomb of a man speaking the language most natural to him:

> I reckon I am their boss, and they make me a pet besides.

> And will go gallivant with the light and air myself.

> Shoulder your duds, dear son, and I will mine.

> Earth! you seem to look for something at my hands,
> Say, old top-knot, what do you want?

One of Whitman's demands in the *Primer* was that words should be brought into literature from factories and farms and trades, for he knew that 'around the markets, among the fish-smacks, along the wharves, you hear a thousand words, never yet printed in the repertoire of any lexicon.' What resulted was sometimes as mechanical as the long lists in 'A Song for Occupations,' but his resolve for inclusiveness also produced dozens of snap-shot impressions as accurate as

> The butcher-boy puts off his killing-clothes, or sharpens his knife at the stall
>   in the market,
> I loiter enjoying his repartee and his shuffle and break-down.

Watching men in action called out of him some of his most fluid phrases, which seem to bathe and surround the objects they describe—as this, of the blacksmiths:

The *lithe sheer* of their waists plays even with their massive arms.

Or this,

The negro holds firmly the reins of his four horses, the block *swags under-neath* on its tied-over chain.

Or a line that is itself a description of the very process by which he enfolds such movement:

In me the caresser of life wherever moving, backward as well as forward *sluing.*

At times he produced suggestive coinages of his own:

The blab of the pave, tires of carts, sluff of boot-soles, talk of the promenaders.

Yet he is making various approaches to language even in that one line. 'Blab' and 'sluff' have risen from his desire to suggest actual sounds, but 'promenad-ers,' which also sounds well, has clearly been employed for that reason alone since it does not belong to the talk of any American folk. 'Pave' instead of 'pavement' is the kind of bastard word that, to use another, Whitman liked to 'promulge.' Sometimes it is hard to tell whether such words sprang from intention or ignorance, particularly in view of the appearance of 'semitic' in place of 'seminal' ('semitic muscle,' 'semitic milk') in both the 1855 preface and first printing of 'A Woman Waits for Me.' Most frequently his hybrids take the form of the free substitution of one part of speech for another—sometimes quite effectively ('the soothe of the waves'), sometimes less so (she that 'birth'd him').

   Although it has been estimated that Whitman had a vocabulary of more than thirteen thousand words, of which slightly over half were used by him only once,[1] the number of his authentic coinages is not very large. Probably the largest group is composed of his agent-nouns, which is not surprising for a poet who was so occupied with types and classes of men and women. Unfortunately these also furnish some of the ugliest-sounding words in his pages, 'originatress,' 'revoltress,' 'dispensatress,' which have hardly been sur-passed even in the age of the realtor and the beautician. He was luckier with an occasional abstract noun like 'presidentiad,' though this is offset by a needless monstrosity like 'savantism.' The one kind of coinage where his ear was listening sensitively is in such compounds as 'the transparent green-shine'

---

1. The reported figures, 13,447 and 6,978, are those of W. H. Trimble's unpublished concor-dance. The most useful work that has been done on Whitman's diction are several articles by Louise Pound, particularly 'Walt Whitman's Neologisms' (*American Mercury*, February 1925) and 'Walt Whitman and the French Language' (*American Speech*, May 1926).

of the water around the naked swimmer in 'I Sing the Body Electric,' or that evoking the apples hanging 'indolent-ripe' in 'Halcyon Days.'

His belief in the need to speak not merely for Americans but for the workers of all lands seems to have given the impetus for his odd habit of introducing random words from other languages, to the point of talking about 'the ouvrier class'! He took from the Italian chiefly the terms of the opera, also 'viva,' 'romanza,' and even 'ambulanza.' From the Spanish he was pleased to borrow the orotund way of naming his countrymen 'Americanos,' while the occasional circulation of Mexican dollars in the States during the eighteen-forties may have given him his word 'Libertad.' His favorite 'camerado,' an archaic English version of the Spanish 'camarada,' seems most likely to have come to him from the pages of the Waverley novels, of which he had been an enthusiastic reader in his youth. But the smattering of French which he picked up on his trip to New Orleans, and which constituted the most extensive knowledge that he ever was to have of another tongue, furnished him with the majority of his borrowings. It allowed him to talk of his 'amour' and his 'eleves,' of a 'soiree' or an 'accoucheur,' of 'trottoirs' and 'feuillage' and 'delicatesse'; to say that his were not 'the songs of an ennuyeed person,' or to shout, 'Allons! from all formules! . . . Allons! the road is before us!' Frequently he was speaking no language, as when he proclaimed himself 'no dainty dolce affetuoso.' But he could go much farther than that into a foreign jargon in his desire to 'eclaircise the myths Asiatic' in his 'Passage to India,' or to fulfil 'the rapt promises and luminé of seers.' He could address God, with ecstatic and monumental tasteless-ness, as 'thou reservoir.'

Many of these are samples of the confused American effort to talk big by using high-sounding terms with only the vaguest notion of their original meaning. The resultant fantastic transformations have enlivened every stage of our history, from the frontiersman's determination to twist his tongue around the syllables of the French settlement at Chemincouvert, Ark., which ended up with the name being turned into Smackover, down to Ring Lardner's dumb nurse who thought people were calling her 'a mormon or something.' In Whitman's case, the fact that he was a reader and so could depend upon letters as well as upon sounds overheard kept him from drifting to such gorgeous lengths. His transformations retain some battered semblance of the original word, which, with the happy pride of the half-educated in the learned term, he then deployed grandly for purposes of his own. Often the attraction for him in the French words ran counter to the identification he usually desired between the word and the thing, since it sprang from intoxication with the mere sound. You can observe the same tendency in some of the jotted lists of his notebooks, 'Cantaloupe. Muskmelon. Cantabile. Cacique City,' or in his shaping such a generalized description of the earth as 'O vast rondure swimming in space.' When caught up by the desire to include the whole universe in his embrace, he could be swept far into the intense inane, chanting in 'Night on the Prairies' of 'immortality and peace':

How plenteous! how spiritual! how resumé!

The two diverging strains in his use of language were with him to the end, for he never outgrew his tendency to lapse from specific images into undifferentiated and lifeless abstractions, as in the closing phrase of this description of his grandfather: 'jovial, red, stout, with sonorous voice and characteristic physiognomy.' In some of his latest poems, *Sands at Seventy,* he could still be satisfied with the merest rhetoric:

Of ye, O God, Life, Nature, Freedom, Poetry.

In his fondness for all his *Leaves,* he seems never to have perceived what we can note in the two halves of a single line,

I concentrate toward them that are nigh, I wait on the door slab,

—the contrast between the clumsy stilted opening and the simple close. The total pattern of his speech is, therefore, difficult to chart, since it is formed both by the improviser's carelessness about words and by the kind of attention to them indicated in his telling Burroughs that he had been 'searching for twenty-five years for the word to express what the twilight note of the robin meant to him.' He also engaged in endless minute revisions of his poems, the purpose of which is often baffling. Although sometimes serving to fuse the syllables into an ampler rhythm, as in the transformation of

Out of the rocked cradle

into one of his most memorable opening lines; they seem almost as likely to add up to nothing more than the dozens of minor substitutions in 'Salut au Monde,' which leave it the flat and formless catalogue that it was in the beginning. . . .

Yet the broken chrysalis of the old restrictions still hangs about Whitman. Every page betrays that his language is deeply ingrained with the educational habits of a middle-class people who put a fierce emphasis on the importance of the written word. His speech did not spring primarily from contact with the soil, for though his father was a descendant of Long Island farmers, he was also a citizen of the age of reason, an acquaintance and admirer of Tom Paine. Nor did Whitman himself develop his diction as Thoreau did, by the slow absorption through every pore of the folkways of a single spot of earth. He was attracted by the wider sweep of the city, and though his language is a natural product, it is the natural product of a Brooklyn journalist of the eighteen-forties who had previously been a country schoolteacher and a carpenter's helper, and who had finally felt an irresistible impulse to be a poet.

From "Whitman," *American Renaissance* (New York: Oxford Univ. Press, 1941), pp. 517-625.

R. W. B. LEWIS

Adam Creates A World

WE RESPOND far less willingly to Whitman's frontal assaults than we do to his dramatizations; when he is enacting his role rather than insisting on it, we are open to persuasion. And he had been enacting it from the outset of *Leaves of Grass.*

This is the true nature of his achievement and the source of his claim to be the representative poet of the party of Hope. For the "self" in the very earliest of Whitman's poems is an individual who is always moving forward. To say so is not merely to repeat that Whitman believed in progress; indeed, it is in some sense to deny it. The young Whitman, at least, was not an apostle of progress in its customary meaning of a motion from worse to better to best, an improvement over a previous historic condition, a "rise of man." For Whitman, there was no past or "worse" to progress from; he moved forward because it was the only direction (he makes us think) in which he could move; because there was nothing behind him—or if there were, he had not yet noticed it. There is scarcely a poem of Whitman's before, say, 1867, which does not have the air of being the first poem ever written, the first formulation in language of the nature of persons and of things and of the relations between them; and the urgency of the language suggests that it was formulated in the very nick of time, to give the objects described their first substantial existence.

Nor is there, in *Leaves of Grass,* any complaint about the weight or intrusion of the past; in Whitman's view the past had been so effectively burned away that it had, for every practical purpose, been forgotten altogether. In his own recurring figure, the past was already a corpse; it was on its way out the door to the cemetery; Whitman watched it absent-mindedly, and turned at once to the living reality. He did enjoy, as he reminds us, reciting Homer while walking beside the ocean; but this was just because Homer was exempt from tradition and talking at and about the dawn of time. Homer was the poet you found if you went back far enough; and as for the sea, it had (unlike Melville's) no sharks in it—no ancient, lurking, indestructible evil powers. Whitman's hope was unspoiled by memory. When he became angry, as he did in *Democratic Vistas* (1871), he was not attacking his generation in the Holgrave manner for continuing to accept the old and the foreign, but for fumbling its extraordinary opportunity, for taking a wrong turn on the bright new highway he had mapped for it. Most of the time he was more interested in the map, and we are more interested in him when he was.

It was then that he caught up and set to music the large contemporary conviction that man had been born anew in the new society, that the race was off to a fresh start in America. It was in *Leaves of Grass* that the optative mood, which had endured for over a quarter of a century and had expressed itself so variously and so frequently, seemed to have been transformed at last into the indicative. It was there that the hope that had enlivened spokesmen from Noah Webster in 1825 ("American glory begins at the dawn") to the well-named periodical, *Spirit of the Age* in 1849 ("The accumulated atmosphere of ages, containing stale ideas and opinions . . . will soon be among the things that were")—that all that stored-up abundance of hope found its full poetic realization. *Leaves of Grass* was a climax as well as a beginning, or rather, it was the climax of a long effort to begin.

This was why Emerson, with whatever enlarged "buts" in his mind, made a point of visiting Whitman in New York and Boston; why Thoreau, refusing to be put off "by an brag or egoism in his book," preferred Whitman to Bronson Alcott; and why Whitman, to the steady surprise of his countrymen, has been regarded in Europe for almost a century as unquestionably the greatest poet the New World has produced: an estimate which even Henry James would come round to. European readers were not slow to recognize in Whitman an authentic rendering of their own fondest hopes; for if much of his vision had been originally imported from Germany and France, it had plainly lost its portion of nostalgia en route. While European romanticism continued to resent the effect of time, Whitman was announcing that time had only just begun. He was able to think so because of the facts of immediate history in America during the years when he was maturing: when a world was, in some literal way, being created before his eyes. It was this that Whitman had the opportunity to dramatize; and it was this that gave *Leaves of Grass* its special quality of a Yankee Genesis: a new account of the creation of the world—the creation, that is, of a new world; an account this time with a happy ending for Adam its hero; or better yet, with no ending at all; and with this important emendation, that now the creature has taken on the role of creator.

It was a twofold achievement, and the second half of it was demanded by the first. We see the sequence, for example, in the development from section 4 to section 5 of "Song of Myself." The first phase was the identification of self, an act which proceeded by distinction and differentiation, separating the self from every element that in a traditional view might be supposed to be part of it: Whitman's identity card had no space on it for the names of his ancestry. The exalted mind which carried with it a conviction of absolute novelty has been described by Whitman's friend, the Canadian psychologist, Dr. R. M. Bucke, who relates it to what he calls Whitman's "cosmic consciousness." "Along with the consciousness of the cosmos [Dr. Bucke wrote], there occurs an intellectual enlightenment which alone would place the individual on a new plane of existence—would make him almost a member of a new species." *Almost a member of a new species:* that could pass as the slogan of each individual in the party of Hope. It was a robust American effort to make real and operative the condition which John Donne once had merely feared:

> Prince, Subject, Father, Son are things forgot,
> For every man alone thinks he has got
> To be a Phoenix and that then can be
> None of that kind, of which he is, but he.

Whitman achieves the freedom of the new condition by scrupulously peel-ing off every possible source of, or influence upon, the "Me myself," the "what I am." As in section 4 of "Song of Myself ":

> Trippers and askers surround me
> People I meet, the effect upon me of my early life, or the
> ward and the city I live in or the nation. . . .
> The sickness of one of my folks, or of myself, or the ill-
> doing or loss or lack of money, or depressions or
> exaltations,
> Battles, the horror of fractricidal wars, the fever of doubtful
> news, the fitful events,
> These come to me days and nights and go from me again,
> But they are not the Me myself.
> Apart from the pulling and hauling stands what I am;
> Stands amused, complacent, compassionating, idle, unitary;
> Looks down, is erect, or bends an arm on an impalpable
> certain rest,
> Looking with side-curved head curious what will come next,
> Both in and out of the game, and watching and wondering
> at it.

There is Emerson's individual, the "infinitely repellent orb." There is also the heroic product of romanticism, exposing behind the mass of what were regard-ed as inherited or external or imposed and hence superficial and accidental qualities the true indestructible secret core of personality. There is the man who contends that "nothing, not God, is greater to one than one's self."

There, in fact, is the new Adam. If we want a profile of him, we could start with the adjectives Whitman supplies: amused, complacent, compassionating, idle, unitary; especially unitary, and certainly very easily amused; too compla-cent, we frequently feel, but always compassionate—expressing the old divine compassion for every sparrow that falls, every criminal and prostitute and hopeless invalid, every victim of violence or misfortune. With Whitman's help we could pile up further attributes, and the exhaustive portrait of Adam would be composed of a careful gloss on each one of them: hankering, gross, mystical, nude; turbulent, fleshy, sensual, eating, drinking, and breeding; no sentimental-ist, no stander above men and women; no more modest than immodest; wearing his hat as he pleases indoors and out; never skulking or ducking or deprecating; adoring himself and adoring his comrades; afoot with his vision,

> Moving forward then and now and forever,
> Gathering and showing more always and with velocity,
> Infinite and omnigenous.

And announcing himself in language like that. For an actual illustration, we could not find anything better than the stylized daguerreotype of himself which Whitman placed as the Frontispiece of the first edition. We recognize him at once: looking with side-curved head, bending an arm on the certain rest of his hip, evidently amused, complacent, and curious; bearded, rough, probably sensual; with his hat on.

Whitman did resemble this Adamic archetype, according to his friend John Burroughs. "There was a look about him," Burroughs remembered, "hard to describe, and which I have seen in no other face,—a gray, brooding, elemental look, like the granite rock, something primitive and Adamic that might have belonged to the first man." The two new adjectives there are "gray" and "brooding"; and they belong to the profile, too, both of Whitman and of the character he dramatized. There was bound to be some measure of speculative sadness inherent in the situation. Not all the leaves Whitman uttered were joyous ones, thought he wanted them all to be and was never clear why they were not. His ideal image of himself—and it is his best single trope for the new Adam—was that of a live oak he saw growing in Louisiana:

> All alone stood it and the mosses hung down from the
>   branches,
> Without any companion it grew there uttering joyous
>   leaves of dark green,
> And its look, rude, unbending, lusty, made me think of
>   myself.

But at his most honest, he admitted, as he does here, that the condition was somehow unbearable:

> I wondered how it could utter joyous leaves standing alone
>   there without a friend near, for I knew I could not. . . .
> And though the live-oak glistens there in Louisiana solitary
>   in a wide flat space,
> Uttering joyous leaves all its life without a friend a lover
>   near,
> I knew very well I could not.

Adam had his moments of sorrow also. But the emotion had nothing to do with the tragic insight; it did not spring from any perception of a genuine hostility in nature or lead to the drama of colliding forces. Whitman was wistful, not tragic. We might almost say that he was wistful because he was not tragic. He was innocence personified. It is not difficult to marshal a vast array of references to the ugly, the gory, and the sordid in his verses; brought together in one horrid lump, they appear as the expression of one who was well informed about the shabby side of the world; but though he offered himself as "the poet of wickedness" and claimed to be "he who knew what it was to be evil," every item he introduced as vile turns out, after all, to be merely a particular beauty of a different original coloration. "Evil propels me and reform of evil propels me, I stand indifferent." A sentiment like that can make sense only if the term "evil" has been filtered through a transfiguring moral imagination, changing in essence as it passes.

That sentiment, of course, is not less an expression of poetic than of moral motivation. As a statement of the poetic sensibility, it could have been uttered as easily by Shakespeare or Dante as by Whitman. Many of the very greatest writers suggest, as Whitman does, a peculiar artistic innocence, a preadolescent wonder which permits such a poet to take in and reproject whatever there is, shrinking from none of it. But in Whitman, artistic innocence merged with moral innocence: a preadolescent ignorance of the convulsive undertow of human behavior—something not at all shared by Dante or Shakespeare. Both modes of innocence are present in the poetry of Walt Whitman, and they are not at any time to be really distinguished. One can talk about his image of moral innocence only in terms of his poetic creation.

"I reject none, accept all, then reproduce all in my own forms." The whole spirit of Whitman is in the line: there is his strategy for overcoming his sadness, and the second large phase of his achievement, following the act of differentiation and self-identification. It is the creative phase, in that sense of creativity which beguiles the artist most perilously into stretching his analogy with God—when he brings a world into being. Every great poet composes a world for us, and what James called the "figure in the carpet" is the poet's private chart of that world, but when we speak of the poet's world—of Dostoevski's or Balzac's—we knowingly skip a phrase, since what we mean is Dostoevski's (or Balzac's) selective embodiment of an already existing world. In the case of Whitman, the type of extreme Adamic romantic, the metaphor gains its power from a proximity to the literal, as though Whitman really were engaged in the stupendous task of building a world that had not been there before the first words of his poem.

The task was self-imposed, for Whitman's dominant emotion, when it was not unmodified joy, was simple, elemental loneliness; it was a testimony to his success and contributed to his peculiar glow. For if the hero of *Leaves of Grass* radiates a kind of primal innocence in an innocent world, it was not only because he had made that world, it was also because he had begun by making himself. Whitman is an early example, and perhaps the most striking one we have, of the self-made man, with an undeniable grandeur which is the product of his manifest sense of having been responsible for his own being—something far more compelling than the more vulgar version of the rugged individual who claims responsibility only for his own bank account.

And of course he was lonely, incomparably lonely; no anchorite was ever so lonely, since no anchorite was ever so alone. Whitman's image of the evergreen, "solitary in a wide, flat space . . . without a friend a lover near," introduced what more and more appears to be the central theme of American literature, in so far as a unique theme may be claimed for it: the theme of loneliness, dramatized in what I shall later describe as the story of *the hero in space*. The only recourse for a poet like Whitman was to fill the space by erecting a home and populating it with companions and lovers.

Whitman began in an Adamic condition which was only too effectively realized: the isolated individual, standing flush with the empty universe, a primitive moral and intellectual entity. In the behavior of a "noiseless, patient spider," Whitman found a revealing analogy:

> A noiseless, patient spider
> I mark'd, where, on a little promontory, it stood out,
>   isolated,
> Mark'd how, to explore the vacant, vast surrounding,
> It launched forth filament, filament, filament, out of itself,
> Ever unreeling them—ever tirelessly speeding them.

"Out of itself." This is the reverse of the traditionalist attitude that, in Eliot's phrase, "home is where one starts from." Whitman acted on the hopeful conviction that the new Adam started from himself; having created himself, he must next create a home. The given in individual experience was no longer a complex of human, racial, and familial relationships; it was a self in a vacant, vast surrounding. Each simple separate person must forge his own framework anew. This was the bold, enormous venture inevitably confronted by the Adamic personality. He had to become the maker of his own conditions—if he were to have any conditions or any achieved personality at all.

There were, in any case, no conditions to *go back to* —to take upon one's self or to embody. There is in fact almost no indication at all in *Leaves of Grass* of a return or reversion, even of that recovery of childhood detected in *Walden*. Whitman begins after that recovery, as a child, seemingly self-propagated, and he is always going *forth;* one of his pleasantest poems was constructed around that figure. There is only the open road, and Whitman moves forward from the start of it. Homecoming is for the exile, the prodigal son, Adam after the expulsion, not for the new unfallen Adam in the western garden. Not even in "Passage to India" is there a note of exile, because there is no sense of sin ("Let others weep for sin"). Whitman was entirely remote from the view of man as an orphan which motivated many of the stories of Hawthorne and Melville and which underlay the characteristic adventure they narrated of the search for a father. Hawthorne, an orphan himself and the author of a book about England called *Our Old Home*, sometimes sent his heroes to Europe to look for their families; Melville dispatched his heroes to the bottom of the sea on the same mission. This was the old way of posing the problem: the way of mastering life by the recovery of home, though it might require descent to the land of the dead; but Whitman knew the secret of his paternity.

Whitman was creating a world, even though he often sounds as though he were saluting a world that had been lying in wait for him: "Salut au monde." In one sense, he is doing just that, welcoming it, acknowledging it, reveling in its splendor and variety. His typical condition is one of acceptance and absorption; the word which almost everyone who knew him applied to his distinguishing capacity was "absorptive." He absorbed life for years; and when he contained enough, he let it go out from him again. "I . . . accept all, then reproduce all in my own forms." He takes unflagging delight in the reproductions: "Me pleased," he says in "Our old Feuillage"; it is the "what I am." But the pleasure of seeing becomes actual only in the process of naming. It is hard to recall any particular of life and work, of men and women and animals and plants and things, of body and mind, that Whitman has not somewhere named in caressing detail. And the process of naming is for Whitman nothing less than the process of creation. This new Adam is both maker and namer; his innocent pleasure, untouched by humility, is colored by the pride of one who looks on his work and finds it good. The things that are named seem to spring into being at the sound of the word. It was through the poetic act that Whitman articulated the dominant metaphysical illusion of his day and became the creator of his own world.

We have become familiar, a century after the first edition of *Leaves of Grass*, with the notion of the poet as the magician who "orders reality" by his use of language. That notion derived originally from the epochal change—wrought chiefly by Kant and Hegel—in the relation between the human mind and the external world; a change whereby the mind "thought order into" the sensuous mass outside it instead of detecting an order externally existing. Whitman (who read Hegel and who wrote a singularly flatulent poetic reflection after doing so) adapted that principle to artistic creativity with a vigor and enthusiasm unknown before James Joyce and his associates in the twentieth century. What is implicit in every line of Whitman is the belief that the poet *projects* a world of order and meaning and identity into either a chaos or sheer vacuum; he does not *discover* it. The poet may salute the chaos; but he creates the world.

Such a conviction contributed greatly to Whitman's ever enlarging idea of the poet as the vicar of God, as the son of God—as God himself. Those were not new labels for the artist, but they had been given fresh currency in Whitman's generation; and Whitman held to all of them more ingenuously than any other poet who ever lived. He supervised the departure of "the priests" and the arrival of the new vicar, "the divine litteratus"; he erected what he called his novel "trinitas" on the base of "the true son of God, the poet"; he offered himself as a cheerful, divine scapegoat and stage-managed "my own crucifixion." And to the extent that he fulfilled his own demands for *the* poet—as laid down in the Preface to *Leaves of Grass* and in *Democratic Vistas* —Whitman became God the Creator.

This was the mystical side of him, the side which announced itself in the fifth section of "Song of Myself," and which led to the mystical vision of a newly created totality. The vision emerges from those lyrical sweeps through the universe in the later sections of the poem: the sections in which Whitman populated and gave richness and shape to the universe by the gift of a million names. We can round out our picture of Whitman as Adam—both Adam as innocent and Adam as namer—if we distinguish his own brand of mysticism from the traditional variety. Traditional mysticism proceeds by denial and negation and culminates in the imagery of deserts and silence, where the voice and the being of God are the whole of reality. Whitman's mysticism proceeds by expansive affirmation and culminates in plenitude and huge volumes of noise. Traditional mysticism is the surrender of the ego to its creator, in an eventual escape from the limits of names; Whitman's is the expansion of the ego in the act of creation itself, naming every conceivable object as it comes from the womb.

The latter figure is justified by the very numerous references, both by Whitman and by his friends, to his "great mother-nature." We must cope with the remarkable blend in the man, whereby this Adam, who had already grown to the stature of his own maker, was not less and at the same time his own Eve, breeding the human race out of his love affair with himself. If section 5 of "Song of Myself " means anything, it means this: a miraculous intercourse between "you my soul" and "the other I am," with a world as its offspring. How the process worked in his poems can be seen by examining any one of the best of them. There Whitman skilfully brings into being the small world of the particular poem by introducing a few items one by one, linking them together by a variety of devices, running back over them time and again to reinsure their solidity and durability, adding further items and quickly forging the relations between them and the cluster already present, announcing at the end the accomplished whole and breathing over all of it the magical command *to be*.

Take, for example, "Crossing Brooklyn Ferry":

> Flood-tide below me! I see you face to face!
> Clouds of the west—sun there half an hour high—I see
>   you also face to face.
> Crowds of men and women attired in the usual costumes,
>   how curious you are to me!
> On the ferry-boats the hundreds and hundreds that cross,
>   returning home, are more curious to me than you
>   suppose,
> And you that shall cross from shore to shore years hence
>   are more to me, and more in my meditations, than you
>   might suppose.

This is not the song of a *trovatore*, a finder, exposing bit by bit the substance of a spectacle which is there before a spectator looks at it. It is the song of a poet who creates his spectacle by "projecting" it as he goes along. The flood tides, the clouds, the sun, the crowds of men and women in the usual costumes: these exist in the instant they are named and as they are pulled in toward one another, bound together by a single unifying eye through the phrases which apply to them severally ("face to face," "curious to me "). The growth of the world is exactly indicated in the increasing length of the lines; until, in the following stanza, Whitman can observe a "simple, compact, well-join'd scheme." Stabilized in space, the scheme must now be given stabilizing relations in time; Whitman goes on to announce that "fifty years hence, others will see them as they cross, the sun half an hour high" (the phrase had to be repeated) "a hundred years hence, or ever so many hundred years hence, others will see them." With the world, so to speak, a going concern, Whitman is able now to summon new elements into existence: sea gulls, the sunlight in the water, the haze on the hills, the schooners and sloops and ships at anchor, the large and small steamers, and the flags of all nations. A few of the conspicuous elements are blessed and praised, in an announcement (stanza 8) not only of their existence but now rather of the value they impart to one another; and then, in the uninterrupted prayer of the final stanza (stanza 9—the process covers nine stanzas, as though it were nine months) each separate entity is named again as receiving everlasting life through its participation in the whole:

> Flow on river! flow with the flood-tide, and
>   ebb with the ebb-tide!
> Frolic on, crested and scallop-edg'd waves!

And so on: until the mystery of incarnation has been completed.

From "The New Adam: Holmes and Whitman," *The American Adam: Innocence, Tragedy, and Tradition in the Nineteenth Century* (1955; rpt. Chicago: Univ. of Chicago Press, 1958), pp. 28-53.

RANDALL JARRELL

Some Lines from Whitman

WHITMAN, Dickinson, and Melville seem to me the best poets of the 19th Century here in America. Melville's poetry has been grotesquely underestimated, but of course it is only in the last four or five years that it has been much read; in the long run, in spite of the awkwardness and amateurishness of so much of it, it will surely be thought well of. (In the short run it will probably be thought entirely too well of. Melville is a great poet only in the prose of *Moby Dick*.) Dickinson's poetry has been thoroughly read, and well though undifferentiatingly loved—after a few decades or centuries almost everybody will be able to see through Dickinson to her poems. But something odd has happened to the living changing part of Whitman's reputation: nowadays it is people who are not particularly interested in poetry, people who say that they read a poem for what it says, not for how it says it, who admire Whitman most. Whitman is often written about, either approvingly or disapprovingly, as if he were the Thomas Wolfe of 19th Century democracy, the hero of a de Mille movie about Walt Whitman. (People even talk about a war in which Walt Whitman and Henry James chose up sides, to begin with, and in which you and I will go on fighting till the day we die.) All this sort of thing, and all the bad poetry that there of course is in Whitman—for any poet has written enough bad poetry to scare away anybody—has helped to scare away from Whitman most "serious readers of modern poetry." They do not talk of his poems, as a rule, with any real liking or knowledge. Serious readers, people who are ashamed of not knowing all Hopkins by heart, are not at all ashamed to say, "I don't really know Whitman very well." This may harm Whitman in your eyes, they know, but that is a chance that poets have to take. Yet "their" Hopkins, that good critic and great poet, wrote about Whitman, after seeing five or six of his poems in a newspaper review: "I may as well say what I should not otherwise have said, that I always knew in my heart Walt Whitman's mind to be more like my own than any other man's living. As he is a very great scoundrel this is not a very pleasant confession." And Henry James, the leader of "their" side in that awful imaginary war of which I spoke, once read Whitman to Edith Wharton (much as Mozart used to imitate, on the piano, the organ) with such power and solemnity that both sat shaken and silent; it was after this reading that James expressed his regret at Whitman's "too extensive acquaintance with the foreign languages." Almost all the most "original and advanced" poets and critics and readers of the last part of the 19th Century thought Whitman as original and advanced as themselves, in manner as well as in matter. Can Whitman really be a sort of Thomas Wolfe or Carl Sandburg or Robinson Jeffers or Henry Miller—or a sort of Balzac of poetry, whose every part is crude but whose whole is somehow great? He is not, nor could he be; a poem, like Pope's spider, "lives along the line," and all the dead lines in the world will not make one live poem. As Blake says, "all sublimity is founded on minute discrimination," and it is in these "minute particulars" of Blake's that any poem has its primary existence.

To show Whitman for what he is one does not need to praise or explain or argue, one needs simply to quote. He himself said, "I and mine do not convince by arguments, similes, rhymes,/ We convince by our presence." Even a few of his phrases are enough to show us that Whitman was no sweeping rhetorician, but a poet of the greatest and oddest delicacy and originality and sensitivity, so far as words are concerned. This is, after all, the poet who said, "Blind loving wrestling touch, sheath'd hooded sharp-tooth'd touch"; who said, "Smartly attired, countenance smiling, form upright, death under the breast-bones, hell under the skull-bones"; who said, "Agonies are one of my changes of garments"; who saw grass as the "flag of my disposition," saw "the sharp-peak'd farmhouse, with its scallop'd scum and slender shoots from the gutters," heard a plane's "wild ascending lisp," and saw and heard how at the amputation "what is removed drops horribly in a pail." This is the poet for whom the sea was "howler and scooper of storms," reaching out to us with "crooked inviting fingers"; who went "leaping chasms with a pike-pointed staff, clinging to topples of brittle and blue"; who, a runaway slave, saw how "my gore dribs, thinn'd with the ooze of my skin"; who went "lithographing Kronos . . . buying drafts of Osiris"; who stared out at the "little plentiful mannikins skipping around in collars and tail'd coat,/ I am aware who they are, (they are positively not worms or fleas)." For he is, at his best, beautifully witty: he says gravely, "I find I incorporate gneiss, coals, long-threaded moss, fruits, grain, esculent roots,/ And am stucco'd with quadrupeds and birds all over"; and of these quadrupeds and birds "not one is respectable or unhappy over the whole earth." He calls advice: "Unscrew the locks from the doors! Unscrew the doors from their jambs!" He publishes the results of research: "Having pried through the strata, analyz'd to a hair, counsel'd with doctors and calculated close,/ I find no sweeter fat than sticks to my own bones." Everybody remembers how he told the Muse to "cross out please those immensely overpaid accounts,/ That matter of Troy and Achilles' wrath, and Aeneas', Odysseus' wanderings," but his account of the arrival of the "illustrious emigré" here in the New World is even better: "Bluff'd not a bit by drainpipe, gasometer, artificial fertilizers,/ Smiling and pleas'd with palpable intent to stay,/ She's here, install'd amid the kitchenware." Or he sees, like another Breughel, "the mechanic's wife with the babe at her nipple interceding for every person born,/ Three scythes at harvest whizzing in a row from three lusty angels with shirts bagg'd out at their waists,/ The snag-toothed hostler with red hair redeeming sins past and to come"—the passage has enough wit not only (in Johnson's phrase) to keep it sweet, but enough to make it believable. He says:

I project my hat, sit shame-faced, and beg.

Enough! Enough! Enough!
Somehow I have been stunn'd. Stand back!
Give me a little time beyond my cuff'd head, slumbers,
    dreams, gaping,
I discover myself on the verge of a usual mistake.

There is in such changes of tone as these the essence of wit. And Whitman
is even more far-fetched than he is witty; he can say about Doubters, in the
most improbable and explosive of juxtapositions: "I know every one of you,
I know the sea of torment, doubt, despair and unbelief./ How the flukes splash!
How they contort rapid as lightning, with splashes and spouts of blood!" Who
else would have said about God: "As the hugging and loving bed-fellow sleeps
at my side through the night, and withdraws at the break of day with stealthy
tread,/ Leaving me baskets cover'd with white towels, swelling the house with
their plenty"?—the Psalmist himself, his cup running over, would have looked
at Whitman with dazzled eyes. (Whitman was persuaded by friends to hide
the fact that it was God he was talking about.) He says, "Flaunt of the sunshine
I need not your bask—lie over!" This unusual employment of verbs is usual
enough in participle-loving Whitman, who also asks you to "look in my face
while I snuff the sidle of evening," or tells you, "I effuse my flesh in eddies,
and drift it in lacy jags." Here are some typical beginnings of poems: "City
of orgies, walks, and joys. . . . Not heaving from my ribb'd breast only. . . . O
take my hand Walt Whitman! Such gliding wonders! Such sights and sounds!
Such join'd unended links. . . . " He says to the objects of the world, "You have
waited, you always wait, you dumb, beautiful ministers"; sees "the sun and stars
that float in the open air,/ The apple-shaped earth"; says, "O suns—O grass
of graves—O perpetual transfers and promotions,/ If you do not say anything
how can I say anything?" Not many poets have written better, in queerer and
more convincing and more individual language, about the world's *gliding
wonders:* the phrase seems particularly right for Whitman. He speaks of those
"circling rivers the breath," of the "savage old mother incessantly crying,/ To
the boy's soul's questions sullenly timing, some drown'd secret hissing"—ends
a poem, once, "We have voided all but freedom and our own joy." How can
one quote enough? If the reader thinks that all this is like Thomas Wolfe he
is Thomas Wolfe; nothing else could explain it. Poetry like this is as far as
possible from the work of any ordinary rhetorician, whose phrases cascade over
us like suds of the oldest and most-advertised detergent.

   The interesting thing about Whitman's worst language (for, just as few
poets have ever written better, few poets have ever written worse) is how
unusually absurd, how really ingeniously bad, such language is. I will quote
none of the most famous examples; but even a line like *O culpable! I acknowledge.
I expose!* is not anything that you and I could do—only a man with the most
extraordinary feel for language, or none whatsoever, could have cooked up
Whitman's worst messes. For instance: what other man in all the history of

this planet would have said, "I am a habitan of Vienna"? (One has an immediate vision of him as a sort of French-Canadian halfbreed to whom the
Viennese are offering, with trepidation, through the bars of a zoological garden,
little mounds of whipped cream.) And *enclaircise* —why, it's as bad as *explicate!*
We are right to resent his having made up his own horrors, instead of sticking
to the ones that we ourselves employ. But when Whitman says, "I dote on
myself, there is that lot of me and all so luscious," we should realize that we
are not the only ones who are amused. And the queerly bad and merely queer
and queerly good will often change into one another without warning: "Hefts
of the moving world, at innocent gambols silently rising, freshly exuding,/
Scooting obliquely high and low"—not good, but *queer!* —suddenly becomes,
"Something I cannot see puts up libidinous prongs,/Seas of bright juice suffuse
heaven," and it is sunrise.

But it is not in individual lines and phrases, but in passages of some length,
that Whitman is at his best. In the following quotation Whitman has something difficult to express, something that there are many formulas, all bad, for
expressing; he expresses it with complete success, in language of the most
dazzling originality:

> The orchestra whirls me wider than Uranus flies,
> It wrenches such ardors from me I did not know I
>   possess'd them,
> It sails me, I dab with bare feet, they are lick'd by the
>   indolent waves,
> I am cut by bitter and angry hail, I lose my breath,
> Steep'd amid honey'd morphine, my windpipe throttled
>   in fakes of death,
> At length let up again to feel the puzzle of puzzles,
> And that we call Being.

One hardly knows what to point at—everything works. But *wrenches* and *did
not know I possess'd them;* the incredible *it sails me, I dab with bare feet; lick'd by
the indolent; steep'd amid honey'd morphine; my windpipe throttled in fakes of death*
—no wonder Crane admired Whitman! This originality, as absolute in its way
as that of Berlioz' orchestration, is often at Whitman's command:

> I am a dance—play up there! the fit is whirling me
>   fast!
> I am the ever-laughing—it is new moon and twilight,
> I see the hiding of douceurs, I see nimble ghosts
>   whichever way I look,
> Cache and cache again deep in the ground and sea, and
>   where it is neither ground nor sea.
> Well do they do their jobs those journeymen divine,
> Only from me can they hide nothing, and would not

if they could,
I reckon I am their boss and they make me a
pet besides,
And surround me and lead me and run ahead when I
walk,
To lift their sunning covers to signify me with stretch'd
arms, and resume the way;
Onward we move, a gay gang of blackguards! with
mirth-shouting music and wild-flapping pennants
of joy!

If you did not believe Hopkins' remark about Whitman, that *gay gang of blackguards* ought to shake you. Whitman shares Hopkins' passion for "dappled" effects, but he slides in and out of them with ambiguous swiftness. And he has at his command a language of the calmest and most prosaic reality, one that seems to do no more than present:

The little one sleeps in its cradle.
I lift the gauze and look a long time, and silently brush
away flies with my hand.
The youngster and the red-faced girl turn aside up the
bushy hill,
I peeringly view them from the top.
The suicide sprawls on the bloody floor of the bed-
room.
I witness the corpse with its dabbled hair, I note where
the pistol has fallen.

It is like magic: that is, something has been done to us without our knowing how it was done; but if we look at the lines again we see the *gauze, silently, youngster, red-faced, bushy, peeringly, dabbled*—not that this is all we see. "Present! present!" said James; these are presented, put down side by side to form a little "view of life," from the cradle to the last bloody floor of the bedroom. . . .

The enormous and apparent advantages of form, of omission and selection, of the highest degree of organization, are accompanied by important disadvantages—and there are far greater works than *Leaves of Grass* to make us realize this. But if we compare Whitman with that very beautiful poet Alfred Tennyson, the most skillful of all Whitman's contemporaries, we are at once aware of how limiting Tennyson's forms have been, of how much Tennyson has had to leave out, even in those discursive poems where he is trying to put everything in. Whitman's poems *represent* his world and himself much more satisfactorily than Tennyson's do his. In the past a few poets have both formed and represented, each in the highest degree; but in modern times what controlling, organizing, selecting poet has created a world with as much in it as Whitman's, a world that so plainly *is* the world? Of all modern poets he has, quantitatively speaking, "the most comprehensive soul"—and, qualitatively, a most comprehensive and comprehending one, with charities and concessions and qualifications that are rare in any time.

"Do I contradict myself? Very well then I contradict myself," wrote Whitman, as everybody remembers, and this is not naive, or something he got from Emerson, or a complacent pose. When you organize one of the contradictory elements out of your work of art, you are getting rid not just of it, but of the contradiction of which it was a part; and it is the contradictions in works of art which make them able to represent to us—as logical and methodical generalizations cannot—our world and our selves, which are also full of contradictions. In Whitman we do not get the controlled, compressed, seemingly concordant contradictions of the great lyric poets, of a poem like, say, Hardy's "During Wind and Rain"; Whitman's contradictions are sometimes announced openly, but are more often scattered at random throughout the poems. For instance: Whitman specializes in ways of saying that there is in some sense (a very Hegelian one, generally) no evil—he says a hundred times that evil is not Real; but he also specializes in making lists of the evil of the world, lists of an unarguable reality. After his minister has recounted "the rounded catalogue divine complete," Whitman comes home and puts down what has been left out: "the countless (nineteen-twentieths) low and evil, crude and savage . . . the barren soil, the evil men, the slag and hideous rot." He ends another such catalogue with the plain unexcusing "All these—all meanness and agony without end I sitting look out upon./See, hear, and am silent." Whitman offered himself to everybody, and said brilliantly and at length what a good thing he was offering:

> Sure as the most certain sure, plumb in the uprights,
>   well entretied, braced in the beams,
> Stout as a horse, affectionate, haughty, electrical,
> I and this mystery here we stand.

Just for oddness, characteristicalness, differentness, what more could you ask in a letter of recommendation? (Whitman sounds as if he were recommending a house—haunted, but what foundations!) But after a few pages he is oddly different:

> Apart from the pulling and hauling stands what I am,
> Stands amused, complacent, compassionating, idle,
>   unitary,
> Looks down, is erect, or bends an arm on an impalpable
>   certain rest
> Looking with side curved head curious what will come
>   next,
> Both in and out of the game and watching and
>   wondering at it.

Tamburlaine is already beginning to sound like Hamlet: the employer feels uneasily, "Why, I might as well hire myself. . . . " And, a few pages later, Whitman puts down in ordinary-sized type, in the middle of the page, this warning to any *new person drawn toward me:*

> Do you think I am trusty and faithful?
> Do you see no further than this facade, this smooth
>   and tolerant manner of me?
> Do you suppose yourself advancing on real ground
>   toward a real heroic man?
> Have you no thought O dreamer that it may be all
>   maya, illusion?

Having wonderful dreams, telling wonderful lies, was a temptation Whitman could never resist; but telling the truth was a temptation he could never resist, either. When you buy him you know what you are buying. And only an innocent and solemn and systematic mind will condemn him for his contradictions: Whitman's catalogues of evils represent realities, and his denials of their reality represent other realities, of feeling and intuition and desire. If he is faithless to logic, to Reality As It Is—whatever that is—he is faithful to the feel of things, to reality as it seems; this is all that a poet has to be faithful to, and philosophers have been known to leave logic and Reality for it.

Whitman is more coordinate and parallel than anybody, is *the* poet of parallel present participles, of twenty verbs joined by a single subject: all this helps to give his work its feeling of raw hypnotic reality, of being that world which also streams over us joined only by *ands,* until we supply the subordinating conjunctions; and since as children we see the *ands* and not the *becauses,* this method helps to give Whitman some of the freshness of childhood. How inexhaustibly interesting the world is in Whitman! Arnold all his life kept wishing that he could see the world "with a plainness as near, as flashing" as that with which Moses and Rebekah and the Argonauts saw it. He asked with elegiac nostalgia, "Who can see the green earth any more/ As she was by the sources of Time?"—and all the time there was somebody alive who saw it so, as plain and near and flashing, and with a kind of calm, pastoral, Biblical dignity and elegance as well, sometimes. The *thereness* and *suchness* of the world are incarnate in Whitman as they are in few other writers.

They might have put on his tombstone WALT WHITMAN: HE HAD HIS NERVE. He is the rashest, the most inexplicable and unlikely—the most impossible, one wants to say—of poets. He somehow is in a class by himself, so that one compares him with other poets about as readily as one compares *Alice* with other books. (Even his free verse has a completely different effect from anybody else's.) Who would think of comparing him with Tennyson or Browning or Arnold or Baudelaire?—it is Homer, or the sagas, or something far away and long ago, that comes to one's mind only to be dismissed; for sometimes Whitman *is* epic, just as *Moby Dick* is, and it surprises us to be able to use truthfully this word that we have misused so many times. Whitman *is* grand, and elevated, and comprehensive, and real with an astonishing reality, and many other things—the critic points at his qualities in despair and wonder, all method failing, and simply calls them by their names. And the range of these qualities is the most extraordinary thing of all. We can surely say about him, "He was a man, take him for all in all. I shall not look upon his like again"—and wish that people had seen this and not tried to be his like: one Whitman is miracle enough, and when he comes again it will be the end of the world.

I have said so little about Whitman's faults because they are so plain: baby critics who have barely learned to complain of the lack of ambiguity in *Peter Rabbit* can tell you all that is wrong with *Leaves of Grass*. But a good many of my readers must have felt that it is ridiculous to write an essay about the obvious fact that Whitman is a great poet. It is ridiculous—just as, in 1851, it would have been ridiculous for anyone to write an essay about the obvious fact that Pope was no "classic of our prose" but a great poet. Critics have to spend half their time reiterating whatever ridiculously obvious things their age or the critics of their age have found it necessary to forget: they say despairingly, at parties, that Wordsworth is a great poet, and *won't* bore you, and tell Mr. Leavis that Milton is a great poet whose deposition *hasn't* been accomplished with astonishing ease by a few words from Eliot. . . . There is something essentially ridiculous about critics, anyway: what is good is good without our saying so, and beneath all our majesty we know this.

Let me finish by mentioning another quality of Whitman's—a quality, delightful to me, that I have said nothing of. If some day a tourist notices, among the ruins of New York City, a copy of *Leaves of Grass*. and stops and picks it up and reads some lines in it, she will be able to say to herself: "How very American! If he and his country had not existed, it would have been impossible to imagine them."

From "Some Lines from Whitman," *Poetry and the Age* (New York: Random House, 1953), pp. 101-21.

The Poem Itself

RICHARD CHASE

"One's Self I Sing"

THE MAIN ITEM of the 1855 edition of *Leaves of Grass* was, of course, "Song of Myself," the profound and lovely comic drama of the self which is Whitman's best poem and contains in essence nearly all, yet not quite all, there is to *Leaves of Grass*. The comic spirit of the poem is of the characteristic American sort, providing expression for a realism at once naturalistic and transcendental, for the wit, gaiety, and festive energy of all good comedy, and also for meditative soliloquy, at once intensely personal and strongly generic.

One circumstance that contributes to the general spontaneity of "Song of Myself " is, in fact, Whitman's unsuccessful attempt to be an Emersonian or Wordsworthian moralist. In his preface, he wrote that "of all mankind the poet is the equable man. Not in him but off from him things are grotesque or eccentric or fail of their sanity . . . He is the arbiter of the diverse and he is the key. He is the equalizer of his age and land." Whitman tries, indeed, to install himself in his poem on this high moral ground: he will, he says, first regenerate himself by leaving the fallacious artificialities of modern life and getting back to fundamentals; then, having perfected himself as the norm, he will summon all the world to him to be freed of its abnormalities. But although in the poem the self remains pretty much at the center of things, Whitman finds it impossible to accept the idea that it is a norm. To the sententious prophet who "promulges" the normative self, the comic poet and ironic realist keep introducing other, disconcertingly eccentric selves.

> Who goes there? hankering, gross, mystical, nude. . . .

Whoever he is, he is not in a position to utter morality. The self in this poem *is* (to use Lawrence's phrase) "tricksy-tricksy"; it does "shy all sorts of ways" and is finally, as the poet says, "not a bit tamed," for "I too am untranslatable." So that as in all true, or high, comedy, the sententious, the too overtly insisted-on morality (if any) plays a losing game with ironical realism. In the social comedy of Moliere, Congreve, or Jane Austen, moral sententiousness, like other deformities of comportment or personality, is corrected by society. But this attitude is, of course, foreign to Whitman, who has already wished to invite society to correct itself by comparing itself with him and who, furthermore, cannot even sustain this democratic inversion of an aristocratic idea. Whitman's comic poetry deflates pretensions and chides moral rigidity by opposing to them a diverse, vital, indeterminate reality.

"I resist anything better than my own diversity," says Whitman, and this is the characteristic note of "Song of Myself." Not that by referring to "Song of Myself" as a "comic" poem I wish too narrowly to limit the scope of discussion—nor do I suggest in using the term a special theory of Whitman or of American literature. I simply respond to my sense that "Song of Myself" is on the whole comic in tone and that although the poem's comic effects are of universal significance, they often take the specific form of American humor. If one finds "Song of Myself" enjoyable at all, it is because one is conscious of how much of the poem, though the feeling in many of its passages need not perhaps have been comic at all, nevertheless appeals to one, first and last, in its comic aspect. The poem is full of odd gestures and whimsical acts; it is written by a neo-Ovidian poet for whom self-metamorphosis is almost as free as free association, who can write "I am an old artillerist" or "I will go to the bank by the wood, and become undisguised and naked" as easily as he can write:

> Askers embody themselves in me and I am embodied
>   in them,
> I project my hat, sit shame-faced, and beg.

The sense of incongruous diversity is very strong in "Song of Myself," and although one does not know how the sly beggar projecting his hat or the martial patriot is transformed into the "acme of things accomplish'd," and "encloser of things to be" who suddenly says:

> I find I incorporate gneiss, coal, long-threaded moss,
>   fruits, grains, esculent roots,
> And am stucco'd with quadrupeds and birds all over,

one is nevertheless charmed with the transformation.

Whitman conceives of the self, one might say, as James conceives of Christopher Newman in *The American* —as having the "look of being committed to nothing in particular, of standing in an attitude of general hospitality to the chances of life." In other words, the "self" who is the protagonist of Whitman's poem is a character portrayed in a recognizable American way; it illustrates the fluid, unformed personality exulting alternately in its provisional attempts to define itself and in its sense that it has no definition. The chief difference between "Song of Myself" and *The American* is, of course, the difference between the stages on which Whitman and James allow the self to act, James confining the action to his international scene and Whitman opening his stage out into an eventful universe which is a contradictory but witty collocation of the natural and the transcendent, the imperfect and the utopian, the personal and the generic—a dialectic world out of whose "dimness opposite equals advance" and in which there is "always a knot of identity" but "always distinction."

The very scope of Whitman's universe and the large freedom he assumes to move about in it allowed him to appropriate new areas of experience and thus to make of "Song of Myself " the original and influential poem it is. For one thing, this is the first American poem to invade that fruitful ground between lyric verse and prose fiction that so much of modern poetry cultivates, and one may suppose that "Song of Myself " has had at least as much effect on the novel as, let us say, *Moby Dick* or *The Golden Bowl* have had on poetry. The famous lines in Section 8 are, at any rate, both "imagistic" and novelistic:

> The little one sleeps in its cradle;
> I lift the gauze and look a long time, and silently brush
> away flies with my hand.
> The youngster and the red-faced girl turn aside up the
> bushy hill;
> I peeringly view them from the top.
> The suicide sprawls on the bloody floor of the bedroom;
> I witness the corpse with its dabbled hair, I note where
> the pistol has fallen.

It is probably true that more than anyone else, more than Blake or Baudelaire, Whitman made the city poetically available to literature:

> The blab of the pave, tires of carts, sluff of boot-soles,
> talk of the promenaders,
> The heavy omnibus, the driver with his interrogating
> thumb, the clank of the shod horses on the granite
> floor . . .

Such lines as these have been multitudinously echoed in modern prose and poetry, they have been endlessly recapitulated by the journey of the realistic movie camera up the city street. One might argue that Whitman's descriptions of the city made possible T. S. Eliot's *Waste Land.* The horror of Eliot's London, as of Baudelaire's *"cité pleine de rêves,"* is unknown in *Leaves of Grass,* but was not Whitman the first poet, so to speak, who put real typists and clerks in the imaginary city?

There can be no doubt that "Song of Myself " made sex a possible subject for American literature, and in this respect Whitman wrought a great revolution in, for example, his beautiful idyllic scene in which the "handsome and richly drest" woman imagines herself to join the "twenty-eight young men" who "bathe by the shore." In such a passage as this (as Henry Adams was to point out) American literature was moving toward the freedom and inclusiveness that came more naturally to Europeans—to Flaubert, or Chekhov, whose panoramic novelette *The Steppe* includes a similarly idyllic scene of bathing and sexuality. It is sex, too, although of an inverted kind, that allows Whitman to write the following unsurpassable lines in which love is at once so sublimely generalized and perfectly particularized:

> And [I know] that a kelson of the creation is love,
> And limitless are leaves stiff or drooping in the fields,
> And brown ants in the little wells beneath them,
> And mossy scabs of the worm fence, and heap'd stones,
>   elder, mullein and poke-weed.

No summary view of "Song of Myself" would be complete without reference to the elegiac tone of the concluding lines. If, as we have been saying, Whitman's poem is remarkable for its gross inclusive scope, his elegiac verse is a great act of discrimination and nicety. Where else, in the generally grandiose nineteenth-century melodrama of love and death shall we find anything like the delicate precision of these incomparable lines?

> The last scud of day holds back for me;
> It flings my likeness after the rest and true as any, on
>   the shadow'd wilds,
> It coaxes me to the vapor and the dusk.
> I depart as air, I shake my white locks at the runaway
>   sun,
> I effuse my flesh in eddies, and drift it in lacy jags.
> I bequeathe myself to the dirt, to grow from the grass
>   I love;
> If you want me again look for me under your boot-
>   soles.
> You will hardly know who I am or what I mean,
> But I shall be good health to you nevertheless,
> And filter and fibre your blood.
> Failing to fetch me at first keep encouraged,
> Missing me one place, search another,
> I stop somewhere, waiting for you.

As every poet does, Whitman asks us provisionally to accept the imagined world of his poem. It is a fantastic world in which it is presumed that the self can become identical with all other selves in the universe, regardless of time and space. Not without precedent in Hindu poetry, this central metaphor is, as an artistic device, unique in American literature, as is the extraordinary collection of small imagist poems, versified short stories, realistic urban and rural genre paintings, inventories, homilies, philosophizings, farcical episodes, confessions, and lyric musings it encompasses in "Song of Myself." Yet as heavily taxing our powers of provisional credence, as inventing a highly idiosyncratic and illusory world, "Song of Myself" invites comparison with other curious works of the American imagination—*Moby Dick,* let us say, and *The Scarlet Letter* and *The Wings of the Dove.* It is of the first importance at any rate to see that Whitman's relation of the self to the rest of the Universe is a successful aesthetic or compositional device, whatever we may think of it as a moral assertion.

If we look at Whitman's implicit metaphor more closely, we see that it consists in the paradox of "identity." The opening words of *Leaves of Grass,* placed there in 1867, state the paradox:

> One's-self I sing, a simple separate person,
> Yet utter the word Democratic, the word En-Masse.

In more general terms the opening lines of "Song of Myself" state the same paradox:

> I celebrate myself and sing myself;
> And what I assume you shall assume;
> For every atom belonging to me, as good belongs
> to you.

Both politically and by nature man has "identity," in two senses of the word: on the one hand, he is integral in himself, unique, and separate; on the other hand, he is equal to, or even the same as, everyone else. Like the Concord transcendentalists, Whitman was easily led in prophetic moods to generalize the second term of the paradox of identity beyond the merely human world and with his ruthless equalitarianism to conceive the All, a vast cosmic democracy, placid, without episode, separation or conflict, though suffused, perhaps, with a bland illumination. More than anything else, it is this latter tendency which finally ruined Whitman as a poet, submerging as it did, his chief forte and glory—his entirely original, vividly realistic presentation of the comedy and pathos of "the simple separate person."

What finally happens is that Whitman loses his sense that his metaphor of self vs. en-masse is a *paradox,* that self and en-masse are in dialectic opposition. When this sense is lost the spontaneously eventful, flowing, and largely indeterminate universe of "Song of Myself" is replaced by a universe that is both mechanical and vaguely abstract. Whatever, in this universe, is in a state of becoming is moving toward the All, and the self becomes merely the vehicle by which the journey is made.

In some of his best as well as in some of his worst poems, Whitman actually conceives of the self as making a journey—for example, "Song of the Open Road," "Crossing Brooklyn Ferry," and "Passage to India." In others the self journeys, as it were, not forward and outward but backward and inward, back to the roots of its being, and discovers there a final mystery, or love, comradeship, or death—for example, the *Calamus* and *Sea Drift* poems. (Notably among the latter are "Out of the Cradle Endlessly Rocking" and "As I Ebb'd with the Ocean of Life".) In "Song of Myself," however, the self is not felt to be incomplete; it has no questing odyssey to make. It stands aggressively at the center of things, "Sure as the most certain sure, plumb in the uprights, well entretied, braced in the beams." It summons the universe, "syphons" universal experience through its dilating pores, calls "anything back again when I desire it." Or the self imagines itself to be infinitely expandable and contractible (like the web of the spider in Whitman's little poem called "A Noiseless Patient

Spider"), so that there is no place where at any moment it may not be, no thing or person with whom it may not merge, no act in which it may not participate. Of great importance is the fact that most of "Song of Myself" has to do not with the self searching for a final identity but with the self escaping a series of identities which threaten to destroy its lively and various spontaneity. This combination of attitudes is what gives "Song of Myself" the alternately ecstatic and gravely musing, pastoral-godlike stability one feels at the center, around which, however, the poet is able to weave the most astonishing embellishments of wit and lyric song. . . .

The motif of "Song of Myself" is the self taking on a bewildering variety of identities and with a truly virtuoso agility extricating itself from each one. The poem begins with the exhortation to leave the "rooms full of perfume," the "creeds and schools." Apart from conventions,

> Apart from the pulling and hauling stands what I am,
> Stands amused, complacent, compassionating, idle, unitary.

Having put society and convention behind, "What I am" finds itself in an Edenlike, early-morning world, wherein one easily observes the portentous dialectics of the universe:

> Urge and urge and urge,
> Always the procreant urge of the world.
> Out of the dimness opposite equals advance, always
> substance and increase, always sex,
> Always a knit of identity, always distinction, always a
> breed of life.

But of more importance is the fact that in this idyllic world the veil is lifted from the jaundiced eye, the cramped sensibility is set free, the senses and pores of the body receive the joyful intelligences dispatched to them by a friendly and providential nature. The self appears to be the offspring of a happy union of body and soul; sublime and delightful thoughts issue from the mind in the same miraculous way as the grass from the ground. Death itself is seen to be "lucky." And, in short, " what I am" can well afford to be complacent, to be certain that it is "unitary." Nor is the feeling of power denied to the self. It derives power from nature, as does the horse—"affectionate, haughty, electrical"—with which the poet compares himself. It derives power, too, from identification with others—the "runaway slave," "the butcher-boy," the "blacksmiths," "the boatmen and clam-diggers," the "trapper," the "red girl"—and finally with America itself.

> In me the caresser of life wherever moving, backward
> as well as forward sluing,
> To niches aside and junior bending, not a person or
> object missing,
> Absorbing all to myself and for this song.

Sections 24-28, though in places rather obscure, contain the essence of Whitman's drama of identity. The poet begins by proclaiming himself a Kosmos, and commanding us to "unscrew the locks from the doors!/ Unscrew the doors themselves from their jambs!" so that the universe may flow through him—"through me the current and index" (that is, the undifferentiated flux and the "identities" that emerge therefrom). This proclamation announces not only the unshakable status and palpable reality but also the redemptive powers of the self. In a world which has been created by banishing social sanctions and social intelligence, what will keep man from being lost in idiocy, crime, squalor? What of that underground realm inhabited by

> . . . the deform'd, trivial, flat, foolish, despised,
> Fog in the air, beetles rolling balls of dung?

The threat of madness, crime, and obscenity is to be allayed by the curative powers of that Adamic world where wisdom consists in uttering "the pass-word primeval," "the sign of democracy." Siphoned through the haughty, electrical self or discussed frankly by persons not inhibited by prudery (the discourses seem perilously interchangeable), the crimes and obscenities will be redeemed:

> Voices indecent by me clarified and transfigur'd.

The poet then records a dreamlike idyl of auto-erotic experience, in which the parts of the body merge mysteriously with natural objects, and a great deal of diffuse and wistful love is generated. And, when dawn comes, the redemption is symbolized in these astonishing metaphors:

> Hefts of the moving world at innocent gambols silently
>   rising, freshly exuding,
> Scooting obliquely high and low.
> Something I cannot see puts upward libidinous prongs,
> Seas of bright juice suffuse heaven.

The poem then speaks anew of how the self may be distorted or destroyed. The poet's "identity" is said to be assailed and warped into other "identities" by agents referred to as "traitors," "wasters," and "marauders." Somewhat elusive in particular, these appear to have in common a quality of aggressiveness and imperiousness. They act as a radical individualist conceives society to act. They break down the self, they swagger, they assert convention, responsibility and reason, they dominate and impose passivity and furtiveness on the individual.

The beautiful, diffuse, kindly dawn is succeeded by a more formidable, a more imperious, apparition. The "dazzling and tremendous" sun leaps over the horizon and cries, "See then whether you shall be master!" The poet replies to this challenge by saying that the sunrise would indeed "kill me/ If I could not now and always send sunrise out of me." The power with which the poet defeats what seeks to destroy him is asserted to be "my vision" and "my voice."

> My voice goes after what my eyes cannot reach,
> With the twirl of my tongue I encompass worlds.

In Section 26 both the metaphorical effects and the subject matter shift from the visual to the auditory. The "bravuras of birds, bustle of growing wheat, gossip of flames, clack of sticks cooking my meals"—these and myriad other sounds amplify into a symphonic orchestration. The crescendo and dying fall of the conclusion are rendered with full tone and exquisite wit.

> I hear the train'd soprano (what work, with hers, is
>   this?)
> The orchestra whirls me wider than Uranus flies,
> It wrenches such ardors from me I did not know I
>   possess'd them,
> It sails me, I dab with bare feet, they are lick'd by the
>   indolent waves,
> I am cut by bitter and angry hail, I lose my breath,
> Steep'd amid honey'd morphine, my windpipe throttled
>   in fakes of death,
> At length let up again to feel the puzzle of puzzles,
> And that we call Being.

But again the poet is confronted with "Being"—that is, form or identity—and is not certain that this is the Being he wants to be. It is therefore dissipated and generalized, in Section 27, into a universal process of reincarnation.

In Section 28 there occurs the famous auto-erotic pastoral dream in which "prurient provokers," like nibbling cows, "graze at the edges of me." The "provokers," conceived as symbolic of the sense of touch, arouse and madden the dreaming poet and then they all unite "to stand on a headland and worry me." After touch has "quivered" him "to a new identity"—has left him confused, vexed, self-reproachful, and isolated—he proceeds in the following sections to resume a "true," "real," or "divine" identity. This act of restoration is accomplished through love, natural piety, pastoral and cosmic meditations, symbolic fusions of self with America, allegations of the "deific" nature of democratic man, ritual celebrations, and fatherly preachments, and finally, in the last Section, by the assertion that death is also merely an extrication of the self from an identity.

From "One's Self I Sing," *Walt Whitman Reconsidered* (New York: William Sloane Associates, 1955), pp. 58-98.

STEPHEN E. WHICHER

"Out of the Cradle Endlessly Rocking"

IN "Out of the Cradle" Whitman has contrived to tell his whole story and even to go beyond it. The long one-sentence "pre-verse" is intended to establish the basic fiction of the poem. The poet will tell us of something long past, he suggests, which now for some reason comes over his memory. By this distancing device he contrives to win some artistic and personal control over his material. In most versions the distinction of the poet that is and the boy that was is made sharp and distinct:

> I, chanter of pains and joys, uniter of here and hereafter . . .
> A reminiscence sing.

Such a bardic line implies firm poetic control, emotion recollected in tranquillity. But neither this line nor the following one is in the 1859 version, where the poet therefore seems much more under the spell of the memories that have seized him:

> A man—yet by these tears a little boy again,
> Throwing myself on the sand, I,
> Confronting the waves, sing.

What has actually seized him, of course, is the meaning *now* to him of these images, so much so that in the first version he has a hard time keeping the presentness of his feelings from bursting through and destroying his narrative fiction.

Nevertheless, the reminiscent mode of the poem greatly enlarges its range by permitting him to bring his whole life to bear on it. As a poem of loss and awakening it goes back even to his very earliest loss and awakening, the "primal" separation of the child from the mother. Though this theme is stressed at once by the poet, especially in the original version, one must avoid reductiveness here. This layer of the poem underlies the whole and already predicts its shape, but it is not the completed structure. From it comes, however, a powerful metaphor for the awakening that is the main subject.

The boy, leaving his bed, finds himself wandering in a strange dark world like something out of Blake, a haunted borderland between shore and sea, here and hereafter, conscious and unconscious. In its troubled restlessness it resembles the moonlit swamp that is glimpsed for a moment in "Song of Myself,"

or some of the dream-scenes in "The Sleepers." We sense here, especially in
the 1859 version, which is more dark and troubled throughout than the final
one, the same dumb, unassuageable grief as in "As I Ebb'd." It also is a
wounded world, impotently twining and twisting with the pain of some
obscure fatality. Here there is even less visible occasion for such agony, since
the chief actor is not a broken poet but a curious child. The poem is heavy
with the man's foreknowledge of what the child, now born, must go through.
Like the star in "When Lilacs Last," however, the scene also has something
to tell, some "drowned secret" which it is struggling to utter. It does not merely
mourn a loss, like the seascape in "As I Ebb'd," but also hints of something
to be found.

What has drawn the boy from his infantile security into this parturient
midnight is a bird. In a flashback the poet tells of the brief May idyll of Two
Together, the sudden loss of the she-bird, and the wonderful song of woe that
followed, drawing the boy back night after night to listen until the night came
when he awakened to its meaning. Then it seemed to him that the bird was
a messenger, an interpreter, singing on behalf of the new world he had entered
to tell him its secret. This secret is really two secrets, that the meaning of life
is love and that he is to be its poet. The song releases the love and the songs
of love in his own heart, which he now realizes has long been ready and waiting
for this moment; he awakes and ecstatically dedicates himself to this service.

Yet, bewilderingly, this discovery of what life means and what he is for at
once plunges him into new trouble and doubt; he finds himself once more
groping for something unknown, and is not released until the voice of the sea
whispers him a very different secret, the word death. This *double* awakening
provides criticism with its chief problem in this poem. It is true that the boy's
spiritual development is dramatically consistent and requires no explanation
from outside the poem, but it is complex and rapid, an extreme example of
dramatic foreshortening. Since it is also intensely personal, the biographical
framework I have sketched helps to make its meaning clear.

To put the matter summarily, in the boy's awakening Whitman has fused
all his own awakenings together, with the result that his poem moves in one
night over a distance which he had taken forty years of life to cover. The
emotional foreground, of course, is occupied by the tragic awakening of 1859,
the discovery of love not merely as a passion for one particular being rather
than an appetite for everything in general, but also as inherently unsatisfied.
Love and grief are one. The bird's story is Whitman's story, distanced and
disguised, but it is also man's. The outsetting bard of love will be the bard
of unsatisfied love because there is no other kind.

But here we encounter a difficulty, for in many of the other poems of 1859
Whitman had suggested that his awakening to love had stopped his poems
and ended his poetic career. Of course he could hardly have overlooked the
fact that his crisis did arouse him to new poems and to some of his best.
Certainly he was proud of this poem, immediately printed it and followed it
with one of his self-written reviews announcing that he would not be mute
any more. Perhaps we may read a special meaning into his selection of this

poem as the first public evidence of his return to song. In this "reminiscence" of the birth of his poetic vocation he is actually celebrating its recovery. The process of relieving his pain in song has now proceeded so far, past "death's outlet" songs like "Hours Continuing Long" and "As I Ebb'd," past a poem of first recognition like "Scented Herbage," that he can now begin to see that the deathblow to his old "arrogant poems" is proving to be a lifeblow to new and better if more sorrowful ones, and so for the first time, in the guise of a reminiscence, he can make not just his grief but its transmutation into the relief of song the subject of his singing.

In the measure that he recovers his poetic future he also recovers his past. His sense of returning powers naturally picks up and blends with his memories of that other awakening, whenever and whatever it was, that led to the poems of 1855. In the boy's joy he draws on and echoes his first awakening, the ecstatic union of self and soul celebrated in "Song of Myself," when he *had* felt a thousand songs starting to life within him in response to the "song of Two Together." Overlaid on that is his second dark awakening to the truth of "two together no more" which had at first appeared to end his singing. If we thus provisionally disentangle the strands that Whitman has woven together we can understand better why the song of the bird must plunge the boy almost simultaneously into ecstasy and despair.

The steps of this process are obscured for us in the final version by Whitman's deletion of a crucial stanza that explains why the boy needs a word from the sea when he already has so much from the bird. After the lines

> O give me some clue!
> O if I am to have so much, let me have more!

the original version continued as follows:

> O a word! O what is my destination?
> O I fear it is henceforth chaos!
> O how joys, dreads, convolutions, human shapes, and all
>   shapes, spring as from graves around me!
> O phantoms! You cover all the land and all the sea!
> O I cannot see in the dimness whether you smile or frown
>   upon me!
> O vapor, a look, a word! O well-beloved!
> O you dear women's and men's phantoms!

This stanza or something similar appears in all editions of "Out of the Cradle" until the last version of 1881, when Whitman was twenty years away from his poem. Perhaps he dropped it then because he felt it spoke too plainly from the emotions of 1859 and was not in keeping with what his poem had become. That it was not necessary to the success of the poem is proved by the success the poem has had without it, yet its omission greatly changes the total effect. The quality of the boy's need is lightened to a more usual adolescent distress and the sea's answer becomes the kind of grave reassurance characteristic of the later Whitman. In the original version the boy is not just distressed, he is desperate with the desperation of the man of 1859. The first act of his awakened poet's vision has been to abort and produce a frightening chaos. Instead of the triumphant vision of Life which Whitman himself had known, when the whole world smiled on its conquering lover, nothing rises now before the outsetting bard but a dim phantasmagoria of death-shapes. It is almost impossible not to read this passage as coming from the poet himself rather than from the boy—indeed, Whitman was right to cut it, it *is* out of keeping—for these "dear women's and men's phantoms" are surely dear because they are those of the men and women and the whole world that had *already* started to life for him in his poems, their life the eddying of his living soul, but are now strengthless ghosts, like the power of vision from which their life had come. This is the "terrible doubt of appearances" that had plagued him from the beginning, now revived and confirmed by his new crisis. Whitman here openly transfers to the boy the man's despair.

With this background it should not be hard to see that the answer the sea gives to the despair characteristic of 1859 is the answer characteristic of 1859. Its essential quality is the same tragic acceptance as in "Scented Herbage," a knowledge of death not as consolation or promise, still less as mere appearance, but as reality, the "real reality" that completes the reality of love in the only way in which it can be completed. In the language of Thoreau, the sea is a "realometer" that says, "this is, and no mistake." The lift her answer brings is like that of "Scented Herbage," the lift of naming the whole truth and so passing beyond illusion to a consent to fate. A sign that this is so is the sea's taciturnity. The thrush's beautiful song of death in 1865, weaving a veil of life-illusion over the same hard truth and so easing it for us, is not present here; simply the word, the thing itself. In this stark directness, again, the kinship is to "Scented Herbage" rather than to "When Lilacs Last."

Yet certainly the fact that this word also, like the bird's song of love and the boy's despair, is ascribed to a dramatic character makes a profound difference. The sea as dramatic character in this poem has two phases. In the earlier part, before the boy turns to her for his answer, she is a background voice blending with the drama of bird and boy but essentially not a part of it. She has an ancient sorrow of her own which leaves her no grief to spare for this small incident on her shores. She does not share the egocentric fallacy of boy and bird, in which even moon, wind, and shadows join in futile sympathy. In this part of the poem she is the same sea as in "As I Ebb'd," the "fierce old mother" who "endlessly cries for her castaways"—all her castaways, not just these—the deep ocean of life and death that rolls through all things.

Of course, behind every detail of the poem, including this one, we feel the poet's shaping power, creating a symbolical language for the life of his own mind. In this kind of subjective drama the author is all the characters; bird, boy, and sea are one and join in a grief that is at bottom the same because it is his own. But Whitman has now seen through the Emersonian illusion that the power of the poet prophesies a victory for the man. Where "Song of Myself" had dramatized the omnipotence of bardic vision, "Out of the Cradle" dramatizes the discovery that the power of the bard is only to sing his own limits. Like the bird in Marianne Moore's poem, his singing is mighty because he is caged. As a dramatic character, then, the sea is the Not-Me, Fate, Karma, that-which-cannot-be-changed. As such she dominates the scene, which is all, as Kenneth Burke would say, under her aegis, but she does not share in its temporal passions.

At the end, however, she condescends to reveal herself and changes from the ground of the question to the answer. The change is not so much in the sea as in the boy. As before, he hears when he is ready to listen; the sea has been speaking all the time. Even the bird, in the early version, heard her and responded with continued song. Before he can hear her the boy must finish his egocentric cycle and pass from his hybristic promise to sing "clearer, louder, and more sorrowful" songs than the bird's to his despairing recognition that there is no good in him. The sign that he is ready is the question itself. Then the sea approaches and whispers as privately for him, revealing the secret which will release him from passion to perception. What she shows him is, I have suggested, no consoling revelation but simply reality. Yet the fact that this answer is now felt to come from the sea, from the heart of the Not-Me that has defeated Whitman's arrogant demands for another Me, suggests that the division between him and his world is not final after all, that the separation both have suffered can still be healed. The elemental forces of "As I Ebb'd" have fused with the perception of reality in "Scented Herbage" to form a new Thou, in Buber's language—no longer the tousled mistress Whitman had ordered around in "Song of Myself," certainly, but a goddess who will speak to him when he is ready to accept her on her own terms. Then he can hear in the voice of the sea the voice of a mother, a figure as we know "always near and always divine" to him. The real reality of "Scented Herbage" has acquired a local habitation and a name, has gathered around itself life and numenosity, and Whitman is well on his way by this dark path to replace the Comrade who had deserted him on the open road.

From "Whitman's Awakening to Death," in *The Presence of Walt Whitman: Selected Papers from the English Institute,* ed. R.W.B. Lewis (New York: Columbia Univ. Press, 1962), pp. 1-27.

CHARLES FEIDELSON, JR.

Symbolism in *"When Lilacs Last in the Dooryard Bloom'd"*

THE PATENT symbols of Whitman's best poem, "When Lilacs Last in the Dooryard Bloom'd," are conditioned by the thoroughgoing symbolism of his poetic attitude. As in most elegies, the person mourned is hardly more than the occasion of the work; but this poem, unlike *Lycidas* or *Adonais,* does not transmute the central figure merely by generalizing him out of all recognition. Lincoln is seldom mentioned either as a person or as a type. Instead, the focus of the poem is a presentation of the poet's mind at work in the context of Lincoln's death. If the true subject of *Lycidas* and *Adonais* is not Edward King or John Keats but the Poet, the true subject of Whitman's "Lilacs" is not the Poet but the poetic process. And even this subject is not treated simply by generalizing a particular situation. The act of poetizing and the context in which it takes place have continuity in time and space but no particular existence. Both are "ever-returning"; the tenses shift; the poet is in different places at once; and at the end this whole phase of creation is moving inexorably forward.

Within this framework the symbols behave like characters in a drama, the plot of which is the achievement of a poetic utterance. The spring, the constant process of rebirth, is threaded by the journey of the coffin, the constant process of death, and in the first section it presents the poet with twin symbols: the perennially blooming lilac and the drooping star. The spring also brings to the poet the "thought of him I love," in which the duality of life and death is repeated. The thought of the dead merges with the fallen star in Section 2; the thought of love merges with the life of the lilac, from which the poet breaks a sprig in Section 3. Thus the lilac and the star enter the poem not as objects to which the poet assigns a meaning but as elements in the undifferentiated stream of thoughts and things; and the spring, the real process of becoming, which involves the real process of dissolution, is also the genesis of poetic vision. The complete pattern of the poem is established with the advent of the bird in the fourth section. For here, in the song of the thrush, the lilac and star are united (the bird sings "death's outlet song of life"), and the potentiality of the poet's "thought" is intimated. The song of the bird and the thought of the poet, which also unites life and death, both lay claim to the third place in the "trinity" brought by spring; they are, as it were, the actuality and the possibility of poetic utterance, which reconciles opposite appearances.

The drama of the poem will be a movement from possible to actual poetic speech, as represented by the "tallying" of the songs of the poet and the thrush.

Although it is a movement without steps, the whole being implicit in every moment, there is a graduation of emphasis. Ostensibly, the visions of the coffin and the star (Sections 5 through 8) delay the unison of poet and bird, so that full actualization is reserved for the end of the poem. On the other hand, the verse that renders the apparition of the coffin *is* "death's outlet song of life." The poetic act of evoking the dark journey is treated as the showering of death with lilac:

> Here, coffin that slowly passes,
> I give you my sprig of lilac. . . .
> Blossoms and branches green to coffins all I bring,
> For fresh as the morning, thus would I chant a song for you,
> O sane and sacred death.

Even as the poet lingers, he has attained his end. And the star of Section 8, the counterpart of the coffin, functions in much the same way. The episode that occurred "a month since"—when "my soul in its trouble dissatisfied sank, as where you sad orb,/ Concluded, dropt in the night, and was gone"—was a failure of the poetic spring. The soul was united with the star but not with the lilac. Yet the passage is preceded by the triumphant statement, "Now I know what you must have meant," and knowledge issues in the ability to render the episode in verse. The perception of meaning gives life to the fact of death; the star meant the death of Lincoln, but the evolution of the meaning is poetry.

The recurrence of the song of the thrush in the following section and in Section 13 is a reminder of the poetic principle which underlies the entire poem. In a sense, the words, "I hear your notes, I hear your call," apply to all that precedes and all that is to come, for the whole poem, existing in an eternal present, is the "loud human song" of the poet's "brother." But again Whitman delays the consummation. He is "detained" from his rendezvous with the bird—although he really "hears" and "understands" all the time—by the sight of the "lustrous star" and by the "mastering odor" of the lilac. Since both the star and the lilac are inherent in the wing of the bird, he actually lingers only in order to proceed. While the song rings in the background, the poet puts the questions presupposed by his own poetizing. How can the life of song be one with the fact of death?—"O how shall I warble myself for the dead one there I loved?" And what will be the content of the song of death?—"O what shall I hang on the chamber walls . . . /To adorn the burial-house of him I love?" The questions answer themselves. The breath by which the grave becomes part of his chant is the breath of life; within the poem the image of the "burial-house" will be overlaid with "pictures of growing spring." The delay has served only to renew the initial theme: the poet's chant, like the song of the thrush, is itself the genesis of life and therefore contains both life and death.

The final achievement of poetic utterance comes in Section 14, when the poet, looking forth on the rapid motion of life, experiences death. More exactly,

he walks between the "thought" and the "knowledge" of death, which move
beside him like companions. Just as his poem exists between the "thought"
of the dead, which is paradoxically an act of life, and the actual knowledge of
the bird's song, which embodies both dying star and living lilac, the poet
himself is in motion from the potential to the actual. From this point to the
end of the poem, the sense of movement never flags. The poet's flight into
the darkness is a fusion with the stream of music from the bird:

> And the charm of the carol rapt me,
> As I held as if by their hands my comrades in the night,
> And the voice of my spirit tallied the song of the bird.

As the motion of the poet is lost in the motion of the song, the latter is
identified with the "dark mother always gliding near," and in the "floating"
carol death itself becomes the movement of waves that "undulate round the
world." In effect, poet and bird, poem and song, life and death, are now the
sheer process of the carol; as in "Out of the Cradle Endlessly Rocking," reality
is the unfolding Word. The presented song merges into the "long panoramas
of visions" in Section 15, and then the inexorable process begins to leave this
moment behind:

> Passing the visions, passing the night,
> Passing, unloosing the hold of my comrades' hands,
> Passing the song of the hermit bird and the tallying song
>   of my soul. . . .
> Passing, I leave thee lilac with heart-shaped leaves, . . .
> I cease from my song for thee, . . .
> O comrade lustrous with silver face in the night.

But the poetic activity is continuous; the passing-onward is not a rejection of
the old symbols. "Lilac and star and bird twined with the chant of . . . [the]
soul" also pass onward because they are activities and not finite things. The
conclusion of this poem dramatizes what Whitman once stated of *Leaves of
Grass* as a whole—that the book exists as "a passage way to something rather
than a thing in itself concluded." Taken seriously, in the sense in which there
can be no "thing in itself concluded," this notion is not, as Whitman sometimes
pretended, a mere excuse for haphazard technique but the rationale of a
symbolistic method.

Yet "When Lilacs Last in the Dooryard Bloom'd" is a successful poem only
because it does not fully live up to the theory which it both states and
illustrates. The poem really presupposes a static situation, which Whitman
undertakes to treat as though it were dynamic; in the course of the poem the
death of Lincoln, of which we always remain aware, is translated into
Whitman's terms of undifferentiated flow. His other long poems generally lack
this stabilizing factor.

From *Symbolism and American Literature* (1956; rpt. Chicago: Univ. of
Chicago Press, 1959), pp. 21-25.

RICHARD P. ADAMS

"Lilacs" As Pastoral Elegy

WHITMAN LIKED to picture himself as an innocent, primitive genius whose "barbaric yawp" was prompted by nature, not culture, and whose originality was ignorant of precedents and uncontaminated by book learning. But modern scholars and critics have shown that he and his art are not so simple as they pretend to be. They are products of a well-advanced artistic and literary development. My purpose is to examine one of his best poems, "When Lilacs Last in the Dooryard Bloom'd," in relation to one of the oldest, most highly respected literary traditions in our civilization—that of pastoral elegy. Everyone knows that "Lilacs" is an elegy, and several writers have compared it in a general way to others, such as "Lycidas," "Adonais," and Emerson's "Threnody."[1] George Meyer of Newcomb College has pointed out the relation of "Lilacs" to pastoral elegy in class lectures, and doubtless others have noticed the same relation in various ways. But no one to my knowledge has made a systematic study of it.

This circumstance, which is rather surprising when we think of it, may be a fair indication of the success with which Whitman covered his cultural tracks. But, by my count, out of seventeen devices commonly used in pastoral elegies from Bion to Arnold,[2] seven appear in "Lilacs." They are the announcement that the speaker's friend or alter ego is dead and is to be mourned; the sympathetic mourning of nature, with the use of the so-called pathetic fallacy; the placing of flowers on the bier; a notice of the irony of nature's revival of life in the spring, when the dead man must remain dead; the funeral procession with other mourners; the eulogy of the dead man; and the resolution of the poem in some formula of comfort or reconciliation.

The other ten, omitted from "Lilacs," are the dramatic framework; the formula "Where were ye, nymphs?"; the inquiry of friends concerning the cause of the speaker's grief; the account of when and how the man died; Echo's lament; the dead man's biography; the pastoral setting; the use of archaisms; the reference to Aphrodite, Urania, or Clio as the dead man's mother or lover; and the account of the dying speech and death.

From Whitman's point of view these ten omissions can be reduced to only

---

1. H. S. Canby, *Walt Whitman* (Boston, 1943), p. 240; James Thomson, *Walt Whitman* (London, 1910), p. 36; and G. W. Allen, *The Solitary Singer* (New York, 1955), p. 341.

2. See G. Norlin,"The Conventions of Pastoral Elegy," *AJP*, XXXII (1911), 296-312, and C. G. Osgood's note in *The Works of Edmund Spenser*, ed. E. Greenlaw et al. (*The Minor Poems*, Baltimore, 1943), I, 399.

two. The first is an avoidance of the literally pastoral element together with all reference to classical mythology. The second is the elimination of any personal reference to the speaker or the dead man that would tend to keep the poem from being about the death of all men. Neither omission damages the fundamental structure or meaning of the traditional elegy, and neither requires to be explained on grounds of ignorance. The first can be accounted to Whitman's bias in favor of the modern over the ancient, and the second to his carefulness never to celebrate the individual at the expense of the general.

Any theory that depended on an assumption of Whitman's ignorance of the conventions of pastoral elegy would be suspect from the start. He must have known "Lycidas," which embodies nearly all of them.[3] He also knew Shelley and referred to him more than once as one of the greatest of English poets.[4] He claimed that he was not well acquainted with Shelley's works,[5] but he admitted on at least one occasion that he was intensely interested in Shelley and Byron as persons if not as poets.[6] He may have minimized his familiarity with Shelley, in somewhat the same way as he did his early knowledge of Emerson, because he had borrowed more heavily from both writers than he wanted to admit in view of his claims to complete originality. This possibility seems especially strong in connection with the 1855 Preface to *Leaves of Grass,* which has a good deal in common with Shelley's "A Defence of Poetry."[7] Whitman was interested enough to clip the "Hymn to Intellectual Beauty" out of an anthology and "To a Skylark" out of some book, probably before 1855.[8] A priori, it seems unlikely that he would not have read "Adonais" by 1865; and there, as in "Lycidas," he would have found almost all the conventions of pastoral elegy as they appear in the older tradition.[9]

Moreover, there are some remarkably specific resemblances in thought and imagery between "Lilacs" and some of the pastoral elegies, notably "Adonais." According to E. R. Wasserman's recent study, the dominant symbols of "Adonais" are light, which is embodied in a star and which represents life, and moisture, which appears as a mist or cloud and which represents death.[10] Whitman associates a star with the living Lincoln and a cloud with Lincoln's death. The star is the same in both poems, Venus, the evening—and also the morning—star. Venus may be the "day-star" of "Lycidas"; it is certainly the "Hesper-Phosphor" which is Tennyson's final symbol of immortality in "In Memoriam." Its meaning is indicated in the epigraph to "Adonais," an aphorism from Plato which Shelley translated,

3. See J. H. Hanford, "The Pastoral Elegy and Milton's *Lycidas,*" *PMLA,* XXV (1910), 409-446.
4. See, e.g., *The Complete Writings of Walt Whitman,* ed. H. L. Traubel et al. (New York, 1902), VI, 289, and VII, 23.
5. H. L. Traubel, *With Walt Whitman in Camden,* II (New York, 1908), 345.
6. *Ibid.,* IV (Philadelphia, 1953), 452.
7. See Allen, p. 156.
8. Allen, p. 127; *Complete Writings,* X, 82 (also p. 67 for another clipping on Shelley).
9. See notes in *Shelley: Selected Poems* . . . , ed. Ellsworth Barnard (New York, 1944), pp. 386-416.
10. *"Adonais:* Progressive Revelation as a Poetic Mode," *ELH,* XXI (Dec. 1954), 282, 292.

> Thou wert the morning star among the living,
> Ere thy fair light had fled;—
> Now, having died, thou art, as Hesperus, giving
> New splendour to the dead.
>
> (BARNARD, p. 386)

These uses of Venus are in harmony with the oldest associations of pastoral elegy. Venus, as the lover of Adonis in Bion's Lament and in the fertility myth that Bion had in mind, represents the principle of life as well as of love and of the rebirth of nature in the spring. Whitman may not have been fully aware of these associations, but he knew that the evening star was Venus and that it was also the morning star, and he must have known the story of Venus and Adonis. Milton, Shelley, and Tennyson were so keenly aware of the classical references that even if Whitman did nothing more than borrow their terms he might be said to have incorporated the ancient fertility myth in his poem.

Whitman's thrush in "Lilacs" has a close resemblance to some of Shelley's birds. In "Adonais" "Thy spirit's sister, the lorn nightingale" associates Keats with the bird which in his own great ode is a prime symbol of immortality. In "A Defence of Poetry" Shelley remarks that "A poet is a nightingale, who sits in darkness and sings to cheer its own solitude with sweet sounds; his auditors are as men entranced by the melody of an unseen musician, who feel that they are moved and softened, yet know not whence or why." And in the poem Whitman clipped and saved, "To a Skylark," the bird is said to be

> Like a poet hidden
> In the light of thought,
> Singing hymns unbidden,
> Till the world is wrought
> To sympathy with hopes and fears it heeded not . . .

Whitman liked to imagine himself, in similar terms, as a singer hidden and alone. He says in "Starting from Paumanok," "Solitary, singing in the West, I strike up for a New World." Addressing the bird in "Out of the Cradle," he says, "O you singer solitary, singing by yourself, projecting me,/O solitary me listening, never more shall I cease perpetuating you . . . " The thrush in "Lilacs" is introduced in the same situation:

> In the swamp in secluded recesses,
> A shy and hidden bird is warbling a song,
>
> Solitary the thrush,
> The hermit withdrawn to himself, avoiding the settlements,
> Sings by himself a song.

In "Adonais" the nightingale is parallel to Echo, who is "a shadow of all sounds," hidden in the mountains, and who "will no more reply to . . . amorous birds," a passage which Shelley borrowed from the Lament for Bion attributed to Moschus. Whitman makes no use of the classical nymph Echo in "Lilacs," but he does speak of "the tallying chant, the echo arous'd in my soul" by the bird's song, which is the substance of his poem.

"Lilacs" is very close to "Adonais" in the use both poets make of the irony of death and the thought or memory of death in the spring. The classical source is again the Lament for Bion: "Ah me, when the mallows wither in the garden, and the green parsley, and the curled tendrils of the anise, on a later day they live again, and spring in another year; but we men, we, the great and mighty, or wise, when once we have died, in hollow earth we sleep, gone down into silence; a right long, and endless, and unawakening sleep."[11] Shelley emphasizes this irony in "Adonais," where he says, "Ah, woe is me! Winter is come and gone,/But grief returns with the revolving year"; and again,

> Nought we know, dies. Shall that alone which knows
> Be as a sword consumed before the sheath
> By sightless lightning?

That is, shall there be conservation of matter and energy, but not of human life? The date of Lincoln's death, 15 April, made a similar emphasis easy and natural in "Lilacs." The lilacs were actually blooming then in Brooklyn, and Whitman remarked later, "By one of those caprices that enter and give tinge to events without being at all a part of them, I find myself always reminded of the great tragedy of that day by the sight and odor of these blossoms. It never fails."[12] His use of lilacs in the poem is not capricious, but functional:

> Ever-returning spring, trinity sure to me you bring,
> Lilac blooming perennial and drooping star in the west,
> And thought of him I love.

The handling of the irony of death and the memory of death in the spring is not explicit; Whitman lets the juxtaposition of images demonstrate it emotionally, or aesthetically, and makes no logical statement about it. But it is the same irony that Shelley found in the Lament for Bion and used in "Adonais."

The reference of lilacs in Whitman's poem is broader than their meaning as representing the rebirth of life in the spring, important as that is. They are also associated more generally, as flowers usually are in the tradition of pastoral elegy, with love. The "heart-shaped leaves" are mentioned three times, and "the perfume strong I love" is related to the leaves before the word "perfume" occurs, twice, in the phrases "what shall my perfume be for the grave of him I love?" and "I'll perfume the grave of him I love." Then the star and "the lilac with mastering odor" hold the speaker back from the attraction of the bird's song until he is joined by "the knowledge of death" and "the thought

---

11. *Theocritus, Bion and Moschus*, tr. A. Lang (London, 1932), p. 201.

12. *Complete Writings*, V, 246 (Whitman's lecture on the death of Lincoln, first given in New York, 14 April 1879).

of death," after which he listens to the song and realizes its meaning and is reconciled. All the major symbols are related in terms of love: the song is of sorrowing love for the dead man, the star is Venus and Venus is the goddess of love, and the lilac is the heart-shaped reminder exuding the mastering odor of love. At the end, as "retrievements out of the night," we are given "Lilac and star and bird twined with the chant of my soul,/ There in the fragrant pines and the cedars dusk and dim." So the associated symbols of love remain in the soul of the singer, in the darkness of death, among the "fragrant" trees.

Shelley also systematically relates his major symbols to the theme of love. His Urania seems to be not only the goddess of astronomy, or the Muse of spiritual poetry, but the Uranian Aphrodite as well, the goddess of spiritual love (Barnard, p. 394). Keats is compared, in an apparent echo from "Lamia," to "a pale flower by some sad maiden cherished,/ And fed with true-love tears, instead of dew." Even the cloud that seems to connote death in "Adonais" as in "Lilacs" is treated as one of Keats's personified Dreams, who, weeping for love of him, melts away. And "the lorn nightingale/ Mourns not her mate with such melodious pain" as loving friends mourn Keats—a treatment that may cause us to wonder if Whitman borrowed from "Adonais" for "Out of the Cradle" as well as for "Lilacs."

These parallels indicate only part of the whole relation of "Lilacs" to the tradition of pastoral elegy. The rest involves some questions of metaphysical meaning and aesthetic value that are much more important than any particular resemblances of wording or imagery. The basic requirement imposed on any elegist, whatever his place in the tradition, is to effect some kind of reconciliation between men's desire for immortality and their knowledge that death is inevitable. The pattern by which this requirement is met is remarkably stable throughout the history of the genre: first, the fact is given that the speaker's friend is dead; second, various other friends mourn with the speaker, and he realizes that death must come to all, including himself; third and last, he is comforted, usually by some assurance or at least suggestion that his friend is immortal in spite of death. The speaker's emotion runs from dismay and sorrow to despair, and thence to hope and often rejoicing.

But the formulas, particularly that of the final consolation, have changed at various points in the course of the tradition. In the fertility cults, comfort was found in the faith that the demigod would be reborn or revived, that the goddess of fertility would rejoice, and that the earth would be replenished in the spring. In the classical elegies, there is usually some indication that the speaker's friend will be given a comparable kind of immortality. Christian elegies nearly always reinforce this pattern with references to the Crucifixion and the Resurrection, holding out the hope of immortality and heaven to all men. In "Lycidas" both formulas are used: the dead man simultaneously becomes an angel in a Christian heaven and a pagan "genius of the shore." Romantic poets tend to modify the formula still further and in an even more radical fashion.

"Adonais" may be said to contain very nearly the whole process and history of this changing tradition. It begins with an almost literal incorporation of the classical point of view, as well as the classical conventions, and then it works almost completely away from both. Most critics have considered this shift a fault, believing that Shelley leaves an unresolved inconsistency, or even a contradiction of views. But Wasserman persuasively argues that the structure of "Adonais" is progressive, in that it presents two inadequate ways of understanding death and immortality before arriving at the satisfactory one with which it concludes. It may be said in the present context that Shelley uses the old formulas only to reject them, or, more precisely, that he aims to transcend the tradition of pastoral elegy in modern romantic terms. "Adonais" works from the classical mode and imagery into a romantic statement of the meaning of life, death, and immortality.

This development involves, among other changes, a shift of emphasis away from the allegorical method used in both pagan and Christian elegies, and tends to erase the distinction carefully made by humanist poets between mind and matter, or between the human individual and the universe. Romantic poets emphasize instead the relations, affinities, and sympathies they find or imagine between the individual and the environment, both natural and social. In their organic picture of the universe they see the particular organism, such as the human mind or personality, taking its place as one of many functional elements that make up the unified whole. The life of an individual is one aspect of the life of the universe, and it is included in, rather than set apart from, its environment. Accordingly, birth is often regarded as the emergence of an individuality from the greater life of the universe, and death as a reabsorption of that individuality into the living whole. Life is eternal, whether the individual is or not, and the individual life is one among many particular manifestations of the living universal principle. A romantic elegist can hardly avoid expressing some attitude, opinion, or feeling about this doctrine.

Wordsworth, for example, in the Immortality Ode (although that poem is not formally an elegy) appears to reason that, because we feel our relation to nature more keenly when we are young than when we are old, we must have had a purer relation before birth than afterward to the principle of life that pervades the universe; therefore we may expect to return to the prenatal relation after we die. Shelley, in "Adonais," says that Keats has been assimilated, "made one with Nature," by "the one Spirit's plastic stress" which gives all things their shape and beauty. This Coleridgean use of the word "plastic" indicates that Shelley has in mind the organic metaphor of the romantics, rather than the Platonic archetype, as the structural principle in terms of which Keats's spirit is assimilated to the spirit of nature. The same formula seems to underlie the imagery by means of which Arnold suggests, in "Thyrsis," that because the elm tree remains to assure him of the Scholar-Gypsy's continued life and quest for knowledge, he knows that his friend Clough also lives after death in the same eternal search. Tennyson tries emotionally to reject the formula at one point:

> That each, who seems a separate whole,
>   Should move his rounds, and fusing all

> The skirts of self again, should fall
> Remerging in the general Soul,
>
> Is faith as vague as all unsweet . . .

But the final resolution of "In Memoriam" is an acceptance of the idea that the speaker's love is "vaster passion" than before, because his friend's soul in death is "mix'd with God and Nature." In the end "we close with all we loved,/And all we flow from, soul in soul." Emerson, with his usual optimism, finds no difficulty; the "deep Heart" comforts him in "Threnody" by saying that

> When frail Nature can no more,
> Then the Spirit strikes the hour:
> My servant Death, with solving rite,
> Pours finite into infinite.

For Emerson, death is not the end of life but a change that enables life to continue by freeing it from the restrictions of the particular form it happens to take on earth.

Whitman's belief is more complex that Emerson's, but it is equally in the romantic tradition. His plainest expression of it is perhaps the statement in "Crossing Brooklyn Ferry":

> I too had been struck from the float forever held in solution,
> I too had receiv'd identity by my body,
> That I was I knew was of my body, and what I should be I
>   knew I should be of my body.

Whitman is saying, if I understand him correctly, that identity is determined by the organic structure of the material body, which is the soul, which is the form life takes in any individual at any time. Life is eternal, and we are therefore in some sense immortal. As Whitman also says, in "Song of Myself," "All goes onward and outward, nothing collapses,/And to die is different from what any one supposed, and luckier." In "Passage to India" he calls on his soul to "Sail forth—steer for the deep waters only," fearlessly into the seas of death, for "are they not all the seas of God?" Everything to Whitman is life, and all life is divine, and there is nothing to fear from any change, even death. His contemplation of the grass in "Song of Myself " leads him to believe that "there is really no death,/And if ever there was it led forward life, and does not wait at the end to arrest it . . . " In the Preface to the 1876 edition, he reaffirms this conviction, "estimating Death, not at all as the cessation, but as somehow what I feel it must be, the entrance upon by far the greatest part of existence, and something that Life is at least as much for, as it is for itself."

There is no explicit statement in "Lilacs" of Whitman's faith in immortality, but the imagery is consistent with his ideas expressed elsewhere. When the speaker of the elegy has faced and realized the fact of death, as given in the song of the thrush, he finds some comfort in the thought that it is not the dead who suffer but the living. Death is the end of suffering; therefore the song of the thrush and "the tallying song" of the speaker's soul are described as "Victorious song, death's outlet song," and the realization of death is not fearful but reassuring. The very sorrow that the speaker feels and the song expresses is one kind of suffering from which the dead man is free. At the same time the sorrow and the song are both contributions to the remembrance of "the sweetest, wisest soul of all my days and lands," which is a kind of immortality. By a somewhat paradoxical train of logic, the speaker celebrates and rejoices, not by giving up or forgetting his sorrow but by revaluing it. He does not deny the reality of death, does not say, as most elegists do in one way or another, "He is not dead." Rather he says, "He is dead therefore I rejoice."

The final worth of Whitman's elegy lies more than that of most elegies, I would suggest, in the song itself:

> Song of the bleeding throat,
> Death's outlet song of life, (for well dear brother I know
> If thou wast not granted to sing thou would'st surely die.)

The song, as an expression or "outlet" of feeling, is to some extent a substitute for death in its relief of suffering. But more than that, and more important to us as readers, it is valuable first as a lasting monument to the dead man and our feeling of love and sorrow for him, and second as a beautiful object in its own right, quite aside from any reference to its occasion. The transmutation of experience into art is a mystery that we might not want to explain if we could, but it is a reality we all recognize. In "Lilacs" Whitman made out of death and sorrow and suffering one of the greatest works of literary art thus far produced in America, and by so doing he made himself immortal.

From "Whitman's 'Lilacs' and the Tradition of Pastoral Elegy," *PMLA*, 72 (1957), 479-87.

JAMES E. MILLER, JR.

"India" and
the Soul's Circumnavigation

"Passage to India" is no more *about* its "subject" than "When Lilacs Last in the Dooryard Bloom'd" is *about* Abraham Lincoln. But, as one begins with Lincoln's death in comprehending "Lilacs," so in understanding "Passage to India" one begins with the "great achievements of the present" celebrated in the opening lines: the Suez Canal, the transcontinental railroad, and the trans-oceanic cable. These modern accomplishments furnish the basic impulse from which the poem takes its origin, but the poem goes far beyond them.

The real subject of "Passage to India" is stated explicitly in section 8 of the poem:

> O soul thou pleasest me, I thee,
> Sailing these seas or on the hills, or waking in the night,
> Thoughts, silent thoughts, of Time and Space and Death, like
>   waters flowing,
> Bear me indeed as through the regions infinite.

"Passage to India" is created out of the poet's "silent thoughts" on time and space and death. But the poem is not about these large philosophical problems in some blurred, abstract sense. The structure of the poem reveals a dramatic progression. The nine sections of the poem may be grouped as follows: sections 1-3, space: the earth spanned; sections 4-6, time: the slopes of history; sections 7-9, death: the soul's circumnavigation. "Passage to India" is a dramatization of the poet's voyages through space and time until, at the end, he arrives at his destination outside both. The meditations on space and time lead to mystical insight into death and an affirmation similar to that in "Out of the Cradle Endlessly Rocking" and "When Lilacs Last in the Dooryard Bloom'd."

I. *Sections 1-3. Space: The Earth Spanned*

Emphasis throughout sections 1 through 3 is placed on space as, paradoxical-ly, the annihilator of time. The achievements of the present which the poet sings are man's contemporary achievements in spanning the globe and bringing the heretofore separated worlds together. Three geographical areas, identified by the poet with the three dominant eras of history, are finally linked: Asia with Europe by the Suez Canal; Europe with the New World by the Atlantic

cable; the New World with Asia by the transcontinental railroad. Although
Whitman celebrates in section 1 this mastery of space, he does so by emphasizing that such mastery, which has brought mankind back to the place of its birth
in Asia, constitutes a spiritual return to the past. Although the poet sings his
"days" through singing their material achievement, the greatness of the present
paradoxically lies in the return to the past that the present has made possible.
This past is a past that exists in space rather than in time. The tendency of
the entire first section of the poem is, through exploitation of the modern
miracles that have diminished space, to diminish time, to connect closely and
inseparably past and present. The section concludes with one of the most vivid
of Whitman's metaphors:

> As a projectile form'd, impell'd, passing a certain line, still keeps on,
> So the present, utterly form'd, impell'd by the past.

The impact of this figure demolishes the differences between present and past:
time is conceived as movement through space. What is present was once past
and will be future: all are the projectile that carries within itself its impulse
onward.

Section 2 of "Passage to India" continues the identification of time with
space. The past, "the dark unfathom'd retrospect," eulogized in the opening
section, turns out to be, in section 2, not a temporal but a geographical reference
to Asia and Africa; but the reference is, ultimately, not really geographical but
spiritual: the poet uses the past symbolically to mean "the far-darting beams
of the spirit, the unloos'd dreams" of Asia and Africa. The refrain, which opens
section 2 and, in variations, several subsequent sections and gives the poem its
title, "Passage O soul to India," demonstrates the poet's achievement in iden-
tifying space with time, in merging the two and making them indistinguishable
for the spirit. Some of Whitman's richest imagery appears in his identification
of spirituality with the source of "the deep diving bibles and legends":

> O you fables spurning the known, eluding the hold of the known, mounting
>   to heaven!
> You lofty and dazzling towers, pinnacled, red as roses, burnish'd with gold!

It is the past as the spirituality of long-ago and far-away India that is, paradoxically, reached through the present's shrunken globe. But the main point is that
this spirituality, presumably remote in time and space, is actually confined to
neither but is outside both and is knowable here and now. The first of the two
brief stanzas that close section 2 indicates that the modern miracles the poet
celebrates, resulting in "the distance brought near" and the "lands . . . welded
together," are a part of "God's purpose from the first." In the closing stanza
the poet reveals explicitly why he has chosen to sing "a worship new," a

worship of those captains and engineers and others who have made possible the spanning of the globe, the conquering of space: "in God's name, and for thy sake O soul."

Section 3 is devoted in its entirety to this "worship new," to the celebration of the achievements of the present through the depiction of "tableaus twain." But throughout these two elaborate pictures of material accomplishment the poet insists that their ultimate service is for the soul ("Lo soul for thee of tableaus twain"; "yet thine, all thine O soul, the same"). As the poet has insisted elsewhere, the route to the spiritual lies through the material; in order to get beyond space and time, one must first be embodied within space and time. These two vignettes—one the opening of the Suez Canal, the other a train ride over the New World's western landscape—serve to memorialize these accomplishments in man's mastery over the world's distances and, at the same time, to suggest the possibility of corresponding spiritual accomplishments. Both these tableaus evoke a sense of movement through space. In the first the poet moves from watching the "procession of steamships" through the Suez Canal to a point on one of them: "I mark from on deck the strange landscape, the pure sky, the level sand in the distance." These observations convey a sense of the vastness of space, but it is a space brought to focus in the poet; instead of space shrinking the poet into insignificance, the poet seems to dominate (if not, indeed, to create) the space. Similarly, in the next tableau the poet moves from a point of observation of the train to a point on the train as it moves swiftly across the continent. And the rugged landscape, instead of appearing formidable and unconquerable, seems rather to be within man's power and subject to his wish as the train rushes swiftly across mountain and plain. Such power comes, paradoxically, from the "duplicate slender lines" of the railroad. And the real significance of the road is that it ties "the Eastern to the Western sea" and serves as "the road between Europe and Asia." This first part of the poem closes with a parenthetical exclamation on Columbus' dream—a dream of the past that envisioned the discovery of a passage to India. The poet sees in these modern engineering feats the fulfilment of the dream of Columbus: "The shore thou foundest verifies thy dream." America itself has become a passage to India.

II. Sections 4-6. Time: The Slopes of History

As the first part of "Passage to India" is devoted to the minimizing of space and uses time or the timelessness of time (the presence of the past) to that end, so the second part of the poem is devoted to the minimizing of time and uses a space now vastly reduced and under man's control to this end. Section 4 of the poem is transitional:

> Struggles of many a captain, tales of many a sailor dead,
> Over my mood stealing and spreading they come,
> Like clouds and cloudlets in the unreach'd sky.

These visions of history now stealing over the poet's mood are, significantly, linked by metaphor to space: events of time are like clouds of the "unreach'd sky." Time is equated with space not only in this figure but also in another that immediately follows:

> Along all history, down the slopes,
> As a rivulet running, sinking now, and now again to the surface rising,
> A ceaseless thought, a varied train—lo, soul, to thee, thy sight, they rise.

The ceaseless events of history are here envisioned as a rivulet running down the slopes of a mountain. Time is conceived in spatial images, and the events of time become visible outside time—to the soul. Time as a barrier is destroyed, once it is penetrated as the poet now spiritually penetrates it: all time is spread out before him as on a landscape. One should note that by implication the rivulet of time running down the slope of history must pour eventually into the sea of spirituality—the world of eidolons. The events of history to be singled out by the spiritual eye of the poet are voyages and expeditions, explorations and discoveries, and particularly those that advanced mankind in its steady onward march. Vasco da Gama is the only individual singled out for mention, for it was he who discovered the sea route to India. As section 4 closes, again there is mention of a "purpose vast" and a reminder that the history to be reviewed has resulted in the "rondure of the world at last accomplish'd."

Sections 5 and 6 constitute the poet's spiritual view of the slopes of history. The first of these sections might be described as a poet's eye view of history in contrast with the more orthodox historical view of section 6. Section 5 opens with a vivid picture of the earth:

> O vast Rondure, swimming in space,
> Cover'd all over with visible power and beauty,
> Alternate light and day and the teeming spiritual darkness.

The poet has begun with the beginning, for the earth is here described from the point of view of God. One might even imagine the Creator as standing off to admire his handiwork and examining closely the "manifold grass and waters, animals, mountains, trees" and deciding that they are good, keeping meanwhile to himself his "inscrutable purpose" and "hidden prophetic intention"—which will be revealed in due time after this curious "vast Rondure" is finally spanned by a curious creature called man. The poet seems to identify himself with God as he says, "Now first it seems my thought begins to span thee." Next in this train of events mankind appears on the scene:

> Down from the gardens of Asia descending radiating,
> Adam and Eve appear, then their myriad progeny after them,
> Wandering, yearning, curious, with restless explorations.

This poet's history of the creation of the world and the origin of man comes from the Bible, one of those "deep diving bibles" that India symbolizes, to which a spiritual "passage" has been made possible by modern-day achievements. Throughout all section 5 no realistically "historical" event is related or mentioned. Yet the poet seems to encompass all time in his sweeping view of the world's total existence. After peopling that "vast Rondure" with the "myriad progeny" of Adam and Eve, the poet speculates on the enigmatic relationship of earth and man: " . . . what is this separate Nature so unnatural?/ What is this earth to our affections?" Although no human answer can satisfy man's restless questions, "Yet soul be sure the first intent remains, and shall be carried out." Continuing his sweeping survey of history, the poet passes swiftly from the far-distant past to a distant future. After the explorers and engineers and scientists have done their work and the physical and material are encompassed and stand revealed,

> Finally shall come the poet worthy that name,
> The true son of God shall come singing his songs.

The works of this poet are to accomplish in the spiritual world what the works of the engineers have achieved in the material world. When he appears on the scene,

> All affection shall be fully responded to, the secret shall be told,
> All these separations and gaps shall be taken up and hook'd
> and link'd together,
> The whole earth, this cold, impassive, voiceless earth, shall be
> completely justified.

This poet as the "true son of God" is one of the kind of poets who wrote the "deep diving bibles and legends" of Asia. In hooking and linking the "separations and gaps," he will be doing spiritually what the explorers and scientists have done materially. The purpose for which this son of God "shall double the cape of Good Hope" will be to discover a spiritual India in which "Nature and Man shall be disjoin'd and diffused no more."

Although section 6 lacks the breath-taking sweep from the past into the future of the previous section, the events related are the "actual" events of history. The poet begins, however, with the events of the present, the events of the "year at whose wide-flung door" he sings, the year of the "marriage of continents": "The lands, geographies, dancing before you, holding a festival garland." From this bright, if incongruous, image the poet passes to the remote historic past, and what follows is a fusion of the familiar and the unfamiliar, the Euphrates, Indus, and Ganges, Alexander, Tamerlane, and Marco Polo—all evoke a sense of the swift passage of time. Saved for full treatment is the "sad shade" but "chief histrion," "the Admiral himself." It was Columbus who, in his search for a passage to India, discovered, instead, America, a discovery that constituted an important link in the chain of events that led to the modern spanning of the globe. It was the Genoese's dream that, the poet noted at the end of section 3, was verified by the modern achievement. It is natural that in his brief survey of history the poet should dwell on Columbus' discovery, fame, and misfortunes, his "dejection, poverty, death." Like the first part of the poem (at the end of section 3), this middle part closes with a parenthetical aside to the reader. The poet abandons his historical survey and comments:

> Curious in time I stand, noting the efforts of heroes,
> Is the deferment long? bitter the slander, poverty, death?

For the poet to say almost casually that he stands "in time" is for him to imply his capability of standing outside time. This same careful placement of the poet "in time" as he surveys history's happenings and dwells on Columbus' misfortunes suggests that the "deferment" is only as long as time. Outside time, in eternity, the "seed unreck'd for centuries in the ground" (like the "seed perfection" of "Song of the Universal") will, on "God's due occasion," rise, sprout, and bloom and fill the "earth with use and beauty." When time becomes timeless, the deferment will end in spiritual fulfilment.

III. Sections 7-9. Death: The Soul's Circumnavigation

After the triumph over space in Part I and the mastery of time in Part II, the poet and his soul are ready in Part III to launch a voyage both spaceless and timeless. Throughout section 7 there is the almost ecstatic realization of both the poet and his repressless soul that they may return, go "back, back to wisdom's birth." The highly charged metaphoric language of this section suggests several levels of meaning. That to which the poet and his soul may return might be any one of four—or all four—places. First, there may be a physical "return" to the East, the cradle of mankind. The material spanning of the globe has made such a return possible. Next, there may be a return in spirit to the time of civilization's birth in the Orient. This time, which coincides with the flourishing "realms of budding bibles," is historically valid. Again, there may be a return to "reason's early paradise," "back to wisdom's birth, to innocent intuitions." This time, the time of Adam and Eve, is not historically but mythically or imaginatively valid. Finally, there is the suggestion in such phrases as "the young maturity of brood and bloom" and "fair creation" that the poet and his soul may long to return, if not to the womb, at least to the "time" before birth—a time of pure, innocent, spiritual existence, a world of spirit whence we come and to which we go. The poet and his soul long for the mystic's experience in his union with God—a union in life identical with the union before and after life.

Sections 8 and 9 represent the poet, in excited anticipation of imminent discoveries, exhorting his soul to begin the voyage. There is in these last two sections the fervency of the evangelist, almost a mystical ecstasy:

> O we can wait no longer,
> We too take ship O soul,
> Joyous we to launch out on trackless seas.

This note of urgency and joyousness that opens section 8 rises gradually to its highest emotional pitch at the close of the poem (a poetic technique Whitman has used elsewhere, particularly in "Starting from Paumanok" and "Song of the Open Road"). In section 8 comes the climax of "Passage to India." After comparing himself and his soul to two lovers in restless, reckless exploration, the poet attempts to re-create the mystic's experience of union with God and to convey some impression of the nature of God's divinity. The poet exclaims:

> Bathe me O God in thee, mounting to thee,
> I and my soul to range in range of thee.

This point in the poem might be recognized as the culmination of the poet's imaginative union with God. Immediately following, the poet seems to be groping for language, however inadequate, to embody his apprehension of Deity. In his search for words, the poet moves quickly from metaphor to metaphor: God is "Thou transcendent," "the fibre and the breath," "Light of the light," center of universes—and more:

> Thou mightier centre of the true, the good, the loving,
> Thou moral, spiritual fountain—affection's source—thou reservoir.

But this imaginative apprehension of God does more than bestow impressions of the Deity; it grants the poet insight not only into himself but also into those allegedly complex philosophical concepts of time, space and death, concepts that, in more senses than one, he has in the earlier parts of the poem penetrated. When the poet exclaims, "Swiftly I shrivel at the thought of God," he evokes in his reader a vivid visual impression of his acute sense of insignificance. But it is the physical self that shrivels. The poet says, "I turning, call to thee O soul, thou actual Me." The "actual" poet is his soul, and his soul, instead of shriveling, infinitely expands:

> ... thou gently masterest the orbs,
> Thou matest Time, smilest content at Death,
> And fillest, swellest full the vastnesses of Space.

The soul, because it is eternal, mates with Time, and because it is infinite, swells "full the vastnesses of Space"; having become equal to time and space, having, in a sense, *become* time and space, the poet's real self, his soul, may in its triumph smile "content at Death." Section 8 concludes with the poet, his imaginative mystical experience concluded, speculating on the nature of the real event that lies ahead, when, "the time achiev'd," "the voyage done," he will finally confront God. He imagines the experience—

> As fill'd with friendship, love complete, the Elder Brother found,
> The Younger melts in fondness in his arms.

The use of the image of melting or dissolution, like "Bathe me O God in thee" and the "spiritual fountain" of a few lines before, conforms to the use of water imagery as symbolic of spirituality throughout *Leaves of Grass*. And the paradoxical element in this figure impresses a paradoxical truth: although there is spiritual interfusion and inseparability of the individual soul and the oversoul, both retain their identity—the Elder Brother his and the Younger his.

The entire last section of the poem is given over to a dramatization of the poet's questioning, pleading with, and exhorting his soul. As the previous section envisioned the ecstasy of mystical union with God, section 9 portrays both poet and soul looking forward with supreme faith to the time when death will precipitate a permanent union with the Transcendent. Both bird and ship serve as images: "Are thy wings plumed indeed for such far flights?" And, immediately following: "O soul, voyagest thou indeed on voyages like those?" Flight or voyage, the "passage" is to more than "India": it is to "ye aged fierce enigmas!" and to "ye strangling problems" and to the "secret of the earth and sky!"—as, indeed, we have already learned in the mystical union portrayed in the previous section. As section 9 progresses, the pleading becomes more fervent, the tone more ecstatic, and the poet cries out, "Passage, immediate passage! the blood burns in my veins!" But even in the ecstatic fervency there is order. The poet exclaims:

> Have we not stood here like trees in the ground long enough?
> Have we not grovel'd here long enough, eating and drinking like
>   mere brutes?
> Have we not darken'd and dazed ourselves with books long enough?

The progression in this passage is not chaotic but systematic, from one end of the scale of life to the other, from plant to animal to man. As the poem closes, the exclamations become more frequent, the lines shorter, until, in the last, the hypnotically repeated words suggest complete ecstatic, but spiritual, abandonment: "O farther, farther, farther sail!"

From *A Critical Guide to Leaves of Grass* (Chicago: Univ. of Chicago Press, 1957), pp. 120-29.

SISTER EVA MARY, O.S.F.

Shades of Darkness In *"The Sleepers"*

IN 'The Sleepers,' the poet (Walt Whitman) moves from an empty darkness to a dreamy twilight, from thence to dusk which gives way to 'winter midnight' closely followed by a dark that is 'blank.' Finally, darkness expands in the softness of a heavenly night that contains all shades of darkness and light.

When the poem opens, the poet observes the sleepers as he stands 'in the dark with drooping eyes by the worst-suffering and most restless.[1] This initial association of darkness with earth and the non-dream world, emphasizes the poet's separation from the sleepers. It is a lonely dark. However, as the poet enters the dream world and participates in the individual dreams of the sleepers, this darkness is dissipated:

> Now I pierce the darkness—new beings appear,
> The earth recedes from me into the night. (p. 425)

The world of light fanciful dreams is lit by a soft oriental glow:

> I am ever-laughing—it is now moon and twilight,
> I see the hiding of douceurs, I see nimble ghosts whichever way I look,
> Cache and cache again deep in the ground and sea, and where it is
> neither ground nor sea. (p. 426)

There is a slipping from this level of dream to a deeper one, and a consequent deepening of the twilight into dusk, as the poet becomes the female awaiting her lover:

> I am she who adorn'd herself and folded her hair expectantly,
> My truant lover has come, and it is dark. (p. 426)

Darkness is addressed by the dreamer and takes on both male and female characteristics:

> Double yourself and receive me darkness,

---

1. Walt Whitman, *Leaves of Grass*, Comprehensive Reader's Edition, edited by Harold W. Blodgett and Sculley Bradley (New York, 1965), p. 425. Subsequent references will be referred to by page number in the text.

Receive me and my lover too, he will not let me go without him.

I roll myself upon you as upon a bed, I resign myself to the dusk.

(p. 426)

At first there are three *personae* involved here—the female dreamer, the lover, and darkness who is asked to receive both the female and her lover. However, in the manner of dreams, three melt into two, as Darkness becomes the male lover to whom the female resigns herself. Darkness is no ordinary lover but personifies both sex and death:

Darkness, you are gentler than my lover, his flesh was sweaty and panting,
I feel the hot moisture yet that he left me.

My hands are spread forth, I pass them in all directions.
I would sound up the shadowy shore to which you are journeying.

(p. 427)

In contrast to the hot darkness of the lover, the darkness of death is characterized by a spiritual element and is cool, gentle, and beckons alluringly. The fragile thread of the dream breaks now, and there is a sense of slipping into the dark of confusion:

Be careful darkness! already what was it touch'd me?
I thought my lover had gone, else darkness and he are one,
I hear the heart-beat, I follow, I fade away. (p. 427)

The poet now descends the 'western course' of old age and becomes the sleepless widow. Through her eyes, the poet sees a unique shade of darkness. The 'winter midnight' of the widow is in direct contrast to the dusk of love and death and is described in terms of light:

It is I too, the sleepless widow looking out on the winter midnight,
I see the sparkles of starshine on the icy and pallid earth. (p. 427)

The brittle cold of a dark that is loveless has rarely been so adequately expressed. The dark of old age looks toward the grave, so the poet now becomes a shroud enwrapping a corpse. The dark of the grave is horribly different from that of death:

It is dark here underground—it is not evil or pain here, it is blank here, for reasons. (p. 427)

This 'blank' seems to approach the 'nothingness' of which the existentialists speak. The poet sees the dark that is blank as the nadir of unhappiness which moves him to say:

> (It seems to me that every thing in the light and air ought to be happy,
> Whoever is not in his coffin and the dark grave let him know he has
> enough.) (pp. 427-428)

The claustrophobic dark of the grave gives impetus to a series of pictures portraying the struggle for life, yet the inevitability of death. The 'gigantic swimmer,' the shipwrecked crew, Washington's troops, struggle and succumb to death. Whereas in the dream of the lover the poet saw death as attractive, he now sees life as also being very dear to man. In contrast to the images of life meeting death, is the memory of the red squaw who comes in the light of the *morning* and delights the mother. Yet, the day of life is incomplete— 'toward the middle of the afternoon she went away.' (p. 430) The mother waits for her in vain. There is no night or fulfillment, so the mother's love goes unrequited. This recognition of the imperfection of day initiates the expansion of night which begins in the next section.

In the darkness of night, all the shades of darkness blend and become one. Not only do the dreams and night contain winter and summer, but also autumn with its subtle blend of shades:

> O love and summer, you are in the dreams and in me,
> Autumn and winter are in the dreams. (p. 430)

The expansion of night continues as 'elements merge in the night.' In the catalogue of unions and mergings, the miracle of the night, as of death, is seen in the leveling and restoring of all the sleepers from the most talented to the idiot:

> The antipodes, and every one between this and them in the dark,
> I swear they are averaged now—one is no better than the other,
> The night and sleep have liken'd them and restored them. (p. 431)

The vision of the unique power of the night leads the poet to see heaven in terms of night:

> Peace is always beautiful,
> The myth of heaven indicates peace and night. (p. 431)

All imperfections await the healing power of this heavenly night:

> The twisted skull waits, the watery or rotten blood waits,
> The child of the glutton or venerealee waits long, and the child
> of the drunkard waits long, and the drunkard himself
> waits long. (p. 432)

The miracle of the heavenly night is that it will make all whole again:

The sweatings and fevers stop, the throat that was unsound is sound,
    the lungs of the consumptive are resumed, the poor distress'd
    head is free. (p. 433)

One cannot help but be reminded here of St. John's assertion: 'So you have
sorrow now, but I will see you again and our hearts will rejoice, and no one
will take your joy from you.' (John 16. 22) The heavenly night is but mirrored
in the temporal night of the sleepers. They too pass from the night renewed,
'They pass the invigoration of the night and the chemistry of the night, and
awake.' (p. 433)

The poet also passes from the night. The vision enables the poet to see
darkness and night as symbolizing the fulfillment of the journey of life—the
return home: 'I stay a while away O night, but I return to you again and love
you.' (p. 433) With the attraction, however, there is also a reminder of man's
fear of death: 'Why should I be afraid to trust myself to you?' Immediately
the poet asserts that he is not afraid and gives reasons:

I know not how I came of you and I know not where I go
    with you, but I know I came well and
    shall go well. (p. 433)

This seems to be a strong affirmation of the heavenly night from whence he
came and to which he will return. The affirmation seems even more powerful
than in 'Song of Myself,' because in 'The Sleepers' there is a very realistic
encounter with both the attractive and repulsive aspects of death.

There is the final comparison of the night with the darkness of the womb.
In contrast to the 'rich running day,' this darkness is still and peaceful,
symbolizing the end of the journey. The poet finally proclaims that he will
rise from the temporal night and return to the eternal heavenly night which
he now calls 'mother':

I will stop only a time with the night, and rise betimes,
I will duly pass the day O my mother, and duly return to you. (p. 433)

As one moves through the layers of darkness in 'The Sleepers,' one participates in the confusion of the dream world. However, one does emerge convinced of having experienced night as the microcosm of that macrocosm in
which life and death, love and death, time and eternity merge in mutual
fulfillment and renewal.

From "Shades of Darkness in 'The Sleepers,' "*Walt Whitman Review*, 15
(1969), 187-90.

GAY WILSON ALLEN

Whitman's Short Lyrics

THE THIRD major development in Whitman's art was the short poem. In the first edition there are no short poems, and no good ones in the second. But in the third (1860) we find many brief poems, some of which are excellent. This edition also gives a clue to the reason for Whitman's turning to the shorter form, and his manuscript notes show plainly the model for his new experiments in verse structure.

The best of these shorter poems are found in a group which he calls "Calamus," a somewhat esoteric title derived from the calamus plant, of the Iris family, with lance-shaped leaves, a phallic blossom, and pink, aromatic roots that thrive in bogs and marshes. The symbolism is indicated in the first poem of the group:

> In paths untrodden,
> In the growth by margins of pond-waters,
> Escaped from the life that exhibits itself,
> From all the standards hitherto published, . . .
>
> . . . .
>
> Strong upon me the life that does not exhibit itself, yet
>   contains all the rest
>
> Resolved to sing no songs to-day but those of manly
>   attachment . . .

The symbolism itself is not a new departure, for the calamus plant is only another kind of grass. But the tone, treatment, and poetic structure are a new departure for Whitman. In his manuscripts he refers to these poems as "sonnets," and when we recall the similarity of the "manly attachment" theme present in most of these poems to Shakespeare's sonnets to his male friend, the connection is obvious. Of course an unrhymed poem without definite metre can only resemble a sonnet in its length, concentration, and thematic treatment, and this we do find in the best of these "Calamus" poems, such as the following:

> When I heard at the close of the day how my name had
>   been received with plaudits in the capitol, still it was
>   not a happy night for me that followed;

And else, when I caroused, or when my plans were
accomplished, still I was not happy;
But the day when I rose at dawn from the bed of perfect
health, refreshed, singing, inhaling the ripe breath of
autumn,
When I saw the full moon in the west grow pale and
disappear in the morning light,
When I wandered alone on the beach, and undressing,
bathed, laughing with the cool waters, and saw the sun
rise,
And when I thought how my dear friend my lover was on
his way coming, O then I was happy,
O then each breath tasted sweeter, and all that day my
food nourished me more, and the beautiful day passed
well,
And the next came with equal joy, and with the next at
evening came my friend,
And that night, while all was still, I heard the waters roll
slowly continually up the shores,
I heard the hissing rustle of the liquid and sands, as
directed to me, whispering, to congratulate me,
For the one I love most lay sleeping by me under the same
cover in the cool night,
In the stillness, in the autumn moonbeams, his face was
inclined toward me,
And his arm lay lightly around my breast—And that
night I was happy.

This poem, however, lacks the tight structure of a real sonnet, and in this
characteristic it is a transition to Whitman's mastery of a compact form.

Another group in the 1860 edition, called "Enfans d'Adam" (later "Children
of Adam"), was written, as Whitman's manuscripts show, to balance the
"friendship for men" group with a cluster on the "amative love of woman."
Oddly enough, these do not show the same influence of the traditional sonnet,
being either longer and more diffuse or shorter and more epigrammatic, as in
No. 14:

I am he that aches with love;
Does the earth gravitate? Does not all matter, aching,
attract all matter?
So the body of me to all I meet, or that I know.

But in the first poem in this group Whitman achieved a weight of connota-
tion and an originality of symbolical structure that anticipated the Symbolists
at the end of the century:
To the garden, the world, anew ascending,

Potent mates, daughters, sons, preluding,
The love, the life of their bodies, meaning and being,
Curious, here behold my resurrection, after slumber,
The revolving cycles, in their wide sweep, having brought
    me again,
Amorous, mature—all beautiful to me—all wondrous,
My limbs, and the quivering fire that ever plays through
    them, for reasons, most wondrous;
Existing, I peer and penetrate still,
Content with the present—content with the past,
By my side, or back of me, Eve following,
Or in front, and I following her just the same.

Since Charles Davis and I have already given a detailed explication of this
poem in the Evergreen edition of *Whitman's Poems,* I will merely refer here to
a few of its accomplishments in language and structure. Although the poem
appears to be more regular than Whitman's earlier poems, the whole approach
is oblique—in syntax, rhetoric, and statement. The thought is of the world
(human society) returning ("ascending") to the lost innocence of Eden, especially in sexual matters. But this has not happened, nor is it prophesied. The
situation evoked is hypothetical—like the poet's metaphorical "resurrection"—and both the syntax and the diction support the implied incomple-
tion.

Many critics have thought the anacoluthon, as illustrated here, the result
either of Whitman's ignorance or carelessness, but he used it so many times
and so often with effectiveness that we must assume he used it deliberately.
Another fine example of such use is in "The Dalliance of the Eagles" (1880).
And of course many of the "Drum Taps" poems violate syntax in order to
emphasize the immediacy, the retrospective *presentness* of scene and incident.

The point to be emphasized, however, is that in working on his shorter
poems Whitman gave more attention to diction, word order, cadence, and
finish. Perhaps his failures are as numerous as in his longer poems, but in
"Sparkles from the Wheel," "To a Locomotive in Winter," and "A Noiseless
Patient Spider," to mention only a few, he wrote some of his finest lyrics. The
"Spider" poem, especially, shows superb mastery. The theme is solitude, and
Whitman used the analogy of a spider sitting on a little promontory, surrounded by vacant space, as a parallel to his own human condition. Just as the spider
throws out "filament, filament, filament, out of itself " (the repetitions convey
the "tireless . . . unreeling"), so does his soul spin its gossamer thread into
"measureless oceans of space." But I must quote the whole poem:

    A noiseless patient spider,
    I mark'd where on a little promontory it stood isolated,
    Mark'd how to explore the vacant vast surrounding,
    It launch'd forth filament, filament, filament, out of itself,
    Ever unreeling them, ever tirelessly speeding them.

And you O my soul where you stand,
Surrounded, detached, in measureless oceans of space,
Ceaselessly musing, venturing, throwing, seeking the
   spheres to connect them,
Till the bridge you will need be form'd, till the ductile
   anchor hold,
Till the gossamer thread you fling catch somewhere, O my
   soul.

Notice the difference between "patient noiseless spider" and Whitman's emphatic, deliberately delayed "noiseless patient spider." Throughout the poem the words, the imagery, and the rhythm perfectly fit the spider's action and the poet's almost desperate prayer to "catch somewhere, O my soul." It is a pleading imperative, not a confident exclamation. "Here," as Mark Van Doren has remarked, "is solitude with a vengeance, in vacancy so vast that any soul at its center, trying to comprehend it, looks terribly minute."

The subject and the symbols remind us of Emily Dickinson, and yet it is such a poem as she never wrote. But to think of the comparison is to realize Whitman's great diversity, for no one would ever think of comparing "Song of Myself " to any example of Emily Dickinson's fragile, subtle art. This poem, no less than "Song of Myself," has space empathy on a vast scale, but the one is painted on a mile-long canvas and the other on the gossamer thread of a spider. The two poems show the vast range in the mutations of Walt Whitman's art.

From *Walt Whitman As Man, Poet, and Legend: With A Check List of Whitman Publications, 1945-1960* (Carbondale: Southern Illinois Univ. Press, 1961), pp. 57-62.

Evaluations

D. H. LAWRENCE

Sympathy on the Open Road

WHITMAN IS a very great poet, of the end of life. A very great post-mortem poet, of the transitions of the soul as it loses its integrity. The poet of the soul's last shout and shriek, on the confines of death. *Après moi le déluge.*
But we have all got to die, and disintegrate.
We have got to die in life, too, and disintegrate while we live.
But even then the goal is not death.
Something else will come.

"Out of the cradle endlessly rocking."

We've got to die first, anyhow. And disintegrate while we still live.
Only we know this much: Death is not the *goal.* And Love, and merging, are now only part of the death-process. Comradeship—part of the death-process. Democracy—part of the death-process. The new Democracy—the brink of death. One Identity—death itself.
We have died, and we are still disintegrating.
But IT IS FINISHED.
Consummatum est.
Whitman, the great poet, has meant so much to me. Whitman, the one man breaking a way ahead. Whitman, the one pioneer. And only Whitman. No English pioneers, no French. No European pioneer-poets. In Europe the would-be pioneers are mere innovators. The same in America. Ahead of Whitman, nothing. Ahead of all poets, pioneering into the wilderness of unopened life, Whitman. Beyond him, none. His wide, strange camp at the end of the great high-road. And lots of new little poets camping on Whitman's camping ground now. But none going really beyond. Because Whitman's camp is at the end of the road, and on the edge of a great precipice. Over the precipice, blue distances, and the blue hollow of the future. But there is no way down. It is a dead end.
Pisgah. Pisgah sights. And Death. Whitman like a strange, modern, American Moses. Fearfully mistaken. And yet the great leader.
The essential function of art is moral. Not aesthetic, not decorative, not pastime and recreation. But moral. The essential function of art is moral.
But a passionate, implicit morality, not didactic. A morality which changes the blood, rather than the mind. Changes the blood first. The mind follows later, in the wake.

Now Whitman was a great moralist. He was a great leader. He was a great changer of the blood in the veins of men.

Surely it is especially true of American art, that it is all essentially moral. Hawthorne, Poe, Longfellow, Emerson, Melville: it is the moral issue which engages them. They all feel uneasy about the old morality. Sensuously, passionally, they all attack the old morality. But they know nothing better, mentally. Therefore they give tight mental allegiance to a morality which all their passion goes to destroy. Hence the duplicity which is the fatal flaw in them: most fatal in the most perfect American work of art, *The Scarlet Letter*. Tight mental allegiance given to a morality which the passional self repudiates.

Whitman was the first to break the mental allegiance. He was the first to smash the old moral conception that the soul of man is something "superior" and "above" the flesh. Even Emerson still maintained this tiresome "superiority" of the soul. Even Melville could not get over it. Whitman was the first heroic seer to seize the soul by the scruff of her neck and plant her down among the potsherds.

"There!" he said to the soul. "Stay there!"

Stay there. Stay in the flesh. Stay in the limbs and lips and in the belly. Stay in the breast and womb. Stay there, Oh Soul, where you belong.

Stay in the dark limbs of negroes. Stay in the body of the prostitute. Stay in the sick flesh of the syphilitic. Stay in the marsh where the calamus grows. Stay there, Soul, where you belong.

The Open Road. The great home of the Soul is the open road. Not heaven, not paradise. Not "above". Not even "within". The soul is neither "above" nor "within". It is a wayfarer down the open road.

Not by meditating. Not by fasting. Not by exploring heaven after heaven, inwardly, in the manner of the great mystics. Not by exaltation. Not by ecstasy. Not by any of these ways does the soul come into her own.

Only by taking the open road.

Not through charity. Not through sacrifice. Not even through love. Not through good works. Not through these does the soul accomplish herself.

Only through the journey down the open road.

The journey itself, down the open road. Exposed to full contact. On two slow feet. Meeting whatever comes down the open road. In company with those that drift in the same measure along the same way. Towards no goal. Always the open road.

Having no known direction even. Only the soul remaining true to herself in her going.

Meeting all the other wayfarers along the road. And how? How meet them, and how pass? With sympathy, says Whitman. Sympathy. He does not say love. He says sympathy. Feeling with. Feel with them as they feel with themselves. Catching the vibration of their soul and flesh as we pass.

It is a new great doctrine. A doctrine of life. A new great morality. A morality of actual living, not of salvation. Europe has never got beyond the morality of salvation. America to this day is deathly sick with saviourism. But Whitman, the greatest and the first and the only American teacher, was no

open road, where all men tread. Therefore, I must accept her
of love, or hate, or compassion, or dislike, or indifference. And
ere she takes me, for my feet and my lips and my body are my
ho must submit to her.

itman's message of American democracy.

mocracy, where soul meets soul, in the open road. Democracy.
ocracy where all journey down the open road, and where a soul
ce in its going. Not by its clothes or appearance. Whitman did
. Not by its family name. Not even by its reputation. Whitman
oth discounted that. Not by a progression of piety, or by works
ot by works at all. Not by anything, but just itself. The soul
anced, passing on foot and being no more than itself. And
d passed by or greeted according to the soul's dictate. If it be
t will be worshipped in the road.

f man and woman: a recognition of souls, and a communion of
love of comrades: a recognition of souls, and a communion of
ocracy: a recognition of souls, all down the open road, and a great
its greatness, as it travels on foot among the rest, down the
of the living. A glad recognition of souls, and a gladder worship
greater souls, because they are the only riches.

Merging, brought Whitman to the Edge of Death! Death! Death!
xultance of his message still remains. Purified of MERGING,
YSELF, the exultant message of American Democracy, of souls in
d, full of glad recognition, full of fierce readiness, full of the joy
hen one soul sees a greater soul.

riches, the great souls.

udies in Classic American Literature (1923; rpt. New York: The
Press, 1964), 163-77.

Saviour. His morality was no morality of salvation. His was a morality of the
soul living her life, not saving herself. Accepting the contact with other souls
along the open way, as they lived their lives. Never trying to save them. As
lief try to arrest them and throw them in gaol. The soul living her life along
the incarnate mystery of the open road.

This was Whitman. And the true rhythm of the American continent speaking out in him. He is the first white aboriginal.

"In my Father's house are many mansions."

"No," said Whitman. "Keep out of mansions. A mansion may be heaven
on earth, but you might as well be dead. Strictly avoid mansions. The soul is
herself when she is going on foot down the open road."

It is the American heroic message. The soul is not to pile up defences round
herself. She is not to withdraw and seek her heavens inwardly, in mystical
ecstasies. She is not to cry to some God beyond, for salvation. She is to go down
the open road, as the road opens, into the unknown, keeping company with
those whose soul draws them near to her, accomplishing nothing save the
journey, and the works incident to the journey, in the long life-travel into the
unknown, the soul in her subtle sympathies accomplishing herself by the way.

This is Whitman's essential message. The heroic message of the American
future. It is the inspiration of thousands of Americans to-day, the best souls
of to-day, men and women. And it is a message that only in America can be
fully understood, finally accepted.

Then Whitman's mistake. This mistake of his interpretation of his watch-
word: Sympathy. The mystery of SYMPATHY. He still confounded it with Jesus'
LOVE, and with Paul's CHARITY. Whitman, like all the rest of us, was at the
end of the great emotional highway of Love. And because he couldn't help
himself, he carried on his Open Road as a prolongation of the emotional
highway of Love, beyond Calvary. The highway of Love ends at the foot of
the Cross. There is no beyond. It was a hopeless attempt to prolong the
highway of love.

He didn't follow his Sympathy. Try as he might, he kept on automatically
interpreting it as Love, as Charity. Merging!

This merging, en masse, One Identity, Myself monomania was a carry-over
from the old Love idea. It was carrying the idea of Love to its logical physical
conclusion. Like Flaubert and the leper. The decree of unqualified Charity, as
the soul's one means of salvation, still in force.

Now Whitman wanted his soul to save itself: he didn't want to save it.
Therefore he did not need the great Christian receipt for saving the soul. He
needed to supersede the Christian Charity, the Christian Love, within himself,
in order to give his Soul her last freedom. The high-road of Love is no Open
Road. It is a narrow, tight way, where the soul walks hemmed in between
compulsions.

Whitman wanted to take his Soul down the open road. And he failed in
so far as he failed to get out of the old rut of Salvation. He forced his Soul
to the edge of a cliff, and he looked down into death. And there he camped,
powerless. He had carried out his Sympathy as an extension of Love and

Charity. And it had brought him almost to madness and soul-death. It gave him his forced, unhealthy, post-mortem quality.

His message was really the opposite of Henley's rant:

> "I am the master of my fate,
> I am the captain of my soul."

Whitman's essential message was the Open Road. The leaving of the soul free unto herself, the leaving of his fate to her and to the loom of the open road. Which is the bravest doctrine man has ever proposed to himself.

Alas, he didn't quite carry it out. He couldn't quite break the old maddening bond of the love-compulsion; he couldn't quite get out of the rut of the charity habit—for Love and Charity have degenerated now into habit: a bad habit.

Whitman said Sympathy. If only he had stuck to it! Because Sympathy means feeling with, not feeling for. He kept on having a passionate feeling *for* the negro slave, or the prostitute, or the syphilitic—which is merging. A sinking of Walt Whitman's soul in the souls of these others.

He wasn't keeping to his open road. He was forcing his soul down an old rut. He wasn't leaving her free. He was forcing her into other people's circumstances.

Supposing he had felt true sympathy with the negro slave? He would have felt *with* the negro slave. Sympathy—compassion—which is partaking of the passion which was in the soul of the negro slave.

What was the feeling in the negro's soul?

"Ah, I am a slave! Ah, it is bad to be a slave! I must free myself. My soul will die unless she frees herself. My soul says I must free myself."

Whitman came along, and saw the slave, and said to himself: "That negro slave is a man like myself. We share the same identity. And he is bleeding with wounds. Oh, oh, is it not myself who am also bleeding with wounds?"

This was not *sympathy*. It was merging and self-sacrifice. "Bear ye one another's burdens": "Love thy neighbour as thyself": "Whatsoever ye do unto him, ye do unto me."

If Whitman had truly *sympathized* , he would have said: "That negro slave suffers from slavery. He wants to free himself. His soul wants to free him. He has wounds, but they are the price of freedom. The soul has a long journey from slavery to freedom. If I can help him I will: I will not take over his wounds and his slavery to myself. But I will help him fight the power that enslaves him when he wants to be free, if he wants my help, since I see in his face that he needs to be free. But even when he is free, his soul has many journeys down the open road, before it is a free soul."

And of the prostitute Whitman would have said:

"Look at that prostitute! Her nature has turned evil under her mental lust for prostitution. She has lost her soul. She knows it herself. She likes to make men lose their souls. If she tried to make me lose my soul, I would kill her. I wish she may die."

But of another prostitute he would have said:

"Look! She is fascinated by the F
worn to death by the Priapic usage.
so."

Of the syphilitic he would say:

"Look! She wants to infect all m
And of still another syphilitic:

"Look! She has a horror of her s
her to get cured."

This is sympathy. The soul judg
integrity.

But when, in Flaubert, the man
Bubi de Montparnasse takes the girl
Whitman embraces an evil prostitut
has no desire to be embraced with
won't try to embrace her with love
sympathize with him, you'll loathe it
all men with her syphilis hates you
thize, you'll feel her hatred, and yo
is hate, and you'll share it. Only you
hatred.

The soul is a very perfect judge
dictate to her. Because the mind say:
your soul into kissing lepers or em
of your soul, your body is the body
soul. That is Whitman's message.
Because it *is* a soul, it hates these
therefore to force the body of your s
violation of your soul. The soul wi
deepest will is to preserve its own
mass of disintegrating forces.

Soul sympathizes with soul. And
hates. My soul and my body are on
whole. Only the mind is capable o
drive my soul and body into uncle

What my soul loves, I love.

What my soul hates, I hate.

When my soul is stirred with c

What my soul turns away from

That is the *true* interpretation o
his Sympathy.

And my soul takes the open road
goes along with the souls that are
has sympathy. The sympathy of lo
simple proximity; all the subtle sy
the bitterest hate to passionate lov

It is not I who guide my soul to

soul alon
deep mot
I must g
soul. It is
This is
The tr
American
is known
away with
and Melv
of Charity
passing u
recognized
a great so
The lo
worship.
worship. I
soul seen
common
of great a
Love, a
But the
purified of
the Open
of worship
The on

From
Vikir

ROY HARVEY PEARCE

The Self Against The World

AMERICAN POETRY was born, as it were, in spite of the wishes—at least, the conscious wishes—of those who bore it. In its Puritan stage, it was perhaps not poetry at all, but a possibility for poetry. As a way of imagining and confronting the human situation, it was entailed by the very doctrine and dogma which could allow it only an insignificant place in human affairs. "A little recreation of poetry," as Cotton Mather well knew, could be a dangerous thing, and might itself become one of the "painful studies."

Their poetry is, of all literary forms cultivated by Americans, most surely Puritan in its origins and in its continuing nature. For aside from a single, isolated effort like the seventeenth-century Virginian "Bacon's Epitaph," there *is* no early American poetic imagination except the Puritan.[1] In form, substance, and method, American poetry from the seventeenth century to the present is on the whole a development of the Puritan imagination, with its compulsion to relate, even to make identical, man's sense of his inwardness and his sense of his role in the world at large. The continuity of American poetry moves, as I have said, from Taylor and his kind to Emerson and thence to Whitman. All American poetry since is, in essence if not in substance, a series of arguments with Whitman. In the twentieth century, when poets would set themselves so powerfully against what they felt to be the exhausted "Romanticism" of American poetry thus far, it was above all Whitman whom they chose to oppose; they could forget him only at their great peril. If they battled against Whitman and Whitmanism, the battle—whether or not they could bring themselves to admit it—was on his terms and on his grounds, Puritan-derived and antinomian. So, to look far ahead, the Southerner John Crowe Ransom, at that time participating in this "counter-current" (as Ezra Pound would call it), addressed a Harvard Phi Beta Kappa audience in 1939:

> Plato, before Plotinus gentled him,
> Spoke the Soul's part, and though its vice is known

---

1. Cf. the summary judgment of Louis B. Wright, "Writers of the South," *Literary History of the United States* (New York, 1948), I, 49: "The muse of poetry inspired few Southerners in the colonial period to write from their hearts about their own world. When they wrote verse, the most formalized type of composition, they became self-conscious and imitative." The encyclopedic inventory of Southern writing, Jay Hubbell's *The South in American Literature: 1707-1900* (Durham, N. C., 1954), pp. 3-168, turns up nothing to contradict Mr. Wright's opinion, nor have my own investigations.

We're in his shadow still, and it appears
Your founders most of all the nations held
By his scandal-mongering, and established him.
                    ("Address to the Scholars of New England")

American poetry has thus far lived out its history in the shadow of those
Platonists (Augustinians, Calvinists, Covenant Theologians, witnesses to their
own inwardness as it makes them at once different from and like other men)
who would speak the soul's part: men speaking to men of man. . . .

Whitman is the supremely realized Emersonian poet—the simple, separate
person sufficiently free of theoretical concerns to let his ego roam (or as he put
it, loaf and lean and invite) and endow the world with its utterly human
perfection. Mastering the words which stand for the elements of his world, his
sensibility transforms them into something unmistakably his own, but in the
nature of the transformation does not deny them to other men. Rather, as
though for the first time, it makes them available to other men. Discovering
itself, it would discover the world and reveal it to all comers. Both the preface
to the 1855 *Leaves of Grass* and "By Blue Ontario's Shore," its poetic counterpart, are essentially expansions of "The Poet." And Whitman's conception
of the forms of love whereby one is to discover oneself in myriad aspects of
the cosmos—this is a development of the Emersonian conception of the power
of the poet as universal man. So much is commonplace, part of the system of
assumptions we now regularly take to our reading of Whitman.

A further assumption—following, like the preceding, from an established
fact—is called for: that Emerson's success in celebrating self-reliance, in poems
and out, freed Whitman from the necessity of showing that it might be done.
He had only to do it. His poems—expanding, proliferating, yet ever turning
back in and upon themselves—increased steadily from the 1850's until his last
relatively inactive years. True enough, as he grew older he tried to control,
modulate, even shape their growth; and he was, as studies of the development
of *Leaves of Grass* now claim, successful in this enterprise.[2] But only relatively
successful—since the life of the poems, no matter what he did by way of
revising them, constantly derived from his sense that his obligation was primarily to release the creative self, to make its acts possible in his time, and only
then to shape its working. He may have in the end wanted *Leaves of Grass* to
be a "cathedral." But he could make it into nothing other than a series of
private antinomian chapels, each reflecting a momentary impulse toward structure, each a success in so far as the impulse was carried through. The impulse
was that of the self fully engaged in the act of creating a structure which would
make for the possibility of further creation: an infinite series of those chapels,
as it were—each to be the locale, the occasion, and the means to the creative,
self-assertive, self-discovering act of that infinite number of Americans who

2. Chiefly Gay Wilson Allen, "The Growth of *Leaves of Grass* and the *Prose Works*," *Walt
Whitman Handbook* (Chicago, 1946), pp. 104-227; Frederik Schyberg, *Walt Whitman* (1933), trans.
E. Allen (New York, 1951); Roger Asselineau, *L'Evolution de Walt Whitman Après La Première
Edition des Feuilles D'Herbe* (Paris, 1954); and James Miller, *A Critical Guide to Leaves of Grass*
(Chicago, 1957).

would be drawn into them. The system that Whitman's poetry makes is thus open, however much he may have wanted to close it—to make it a guide to a way of life, not to a way toward life. The effect of Whitman's poems is in the end akin to that of Emerson's. The poet glories in his discovery of the sheer creative, individualizing power of his egocentrism, yet at the same time tries (not quite successfully, I think) to demonstrate somehow that the way into egocentrism is also the way out of it. Emerson had achieved at best a perilous balance here. But his example freed Whitman to be a poet, as it were, beyond balance—a poet who saw that if he were to be a poet, such balance was out of the question. In this may well lie his main claim to glory. In any case, it is at this point, in this light, that Whitman most fully assumes that poetic role set by Emerson's example and demanded by the nature and need of his culture.

In Whitman's poetry, the ego is made not only to assert but to preserve itself. Its tremendous creative powers somehow militate against that fusion of ego and cosmos (that eventual desire to build a cathedral) which seems to have been a major need of the later Whitman. Emphasizing the desire and the need (sharing them, perhaps?), we have too often tended to mistake them for the effect, and also the meaning, of the poetry itself.

The ego asserts itself Adamically, by naming. The poem is a titanic act of adoption. The poet is a father, giving his name to all he sees and hears and feels. His office is to make everything part of the community of man; the sense of community is revealed as he discovers, and then yields to, his infinite sense of himself. He puts things together as they never have been before; they are related only by the force of the poetic ego operative on them. There is little or no dramatic effect in the poems, even those with huge casts of characters; for the items which are named in them do not interact, are not conceived as modifying and qualifying one another, so as to make for dramatic tension. They are referred back to their creator, who does with them as his sensibility wills. If we see a relationship, it is because Whitman has made it, not because it was already there for him to discover and report. The great catalogues are inevitably the principal expressive form for one who would define himself as "Kosmos."

Whitman glories almost exclusively in the first-person singular—and in this a more complete Emersonian than Emerson himself, who trusts it but would discover it explicitly in the third-person too. Whitman said of *Leaves of Grass* that it was the attempt "to put *a Person,* a human being (myself, in the latter half of the Nineteenth Century, in America) freely, fully and truly on record." There can be no third-person in his world; and the second-person must necessarily be at the loving mercy of the first. What is true of *Song of Myself* is true of all the poems: There is no formal control in them but that which stems from the self in the act of revealing the world to itself. For the reader there must be an equivalent experience. As Whitman said of his poems in *A Backward Glance O'er Travel'd Roads* (1888): "I round and finish little, if anything; and could not, consistently with my scheme. The reader will always have his or her part to do, just as much as I have mine."

All experience, all thought, all belief, all appearance are referred back to the ego:

> And I know that the hand of God is the promise of my own,
> And I know that the spirit of God is the brother of my own,
> And that all the men ever born are also my brothers,
>   and the women my sisters and lovers,
> And that a kelson of the creation is love,
> And limitless are leaves stiff or drooping in the fields,
> And brown ants in the little wells beneath them,
> And mossy scabs of the worm fence, heap'd stones,
>   elder, mullein and poke-weed.

Here (the passage is from the fifth section of *Song of Myself*) the world is described as it exists apart from the poet; yet he can name and collocate its potentially infinite aspects only so that he may discover and define his relationship to it. His objectivity is that of an impressionist, and so finally an aspect of his subjectivity. He may aspire to achieve some sort of identity with his world; yet his power of naming, describing, and collocating is such that a reader cannot but be overwhelmingly, even uncritically, aware of the single ego, the self, which generates it. The power is that of a lover who rather drives himself than is drawn to love the world. A Father Adam who bids men listen to him so that they might hear their proper names and so come alive—this is how Whitman images himself. He does not fear his power, but knows that others may. And he must quiet their apprehensions. One short poem says it all:

> As Adam early in the morning,
> Walking forth from the bower refresh'd with sleep,
> Behold me where I pass, hear my voice, approach.
> Touch me, touch the palm of your hand to my body as I pass,
> Be not afraid of my body.

Whitman knew that his fellows *did* live in a paradise, only they could not bring themselves to acknowledge the fact. In that paradise, the soul was the body. In the voice and its use lay proof of their quintessential identity. His subject, as he wrote in a preliminary note for the first section of *Leaves of Grass*, was "Adam, as central figure and type."

But Whitman would go farther than this. Having established the identity of body and soul by expressing it, he would establish higher and more inclusive levels of identity, until his voice should become all voices and all voices become his. Herein lies his special hubris, born of the overconfidence and euphoria which came after he had once and for all discovered his own identity. He did in fact discover his own identity, and he taught other men to discover theirs. But always he was tempted, sometimes fatally, to try to go on and establish a single identity for all—simple, separate, *therefore* democratic, en-masse. He failed. But then: he could not succeed unless he tried to do so much that he inevitably failed.

In "The Sleepers"—to take a great but insufficiently noticed example—the

o admire, "When Lilacs Last in the Dooryard Bloom'd" being the othe
xample. Most of all, it is *structurally* typical of such poems. The structur
of relationship, in which the poet, through his control of two or mor
of view, manages to pull his world together. Yet the relationship is o
cularly limited sort. The points of view are always aspects of the poet'
e self and are manipulated as such; they are in no sense dramatic, much
velistic. Whitman has little or none of that final sense of "otherness"
makes for major fiction. In the end, his poems always return to him as
. This is so because in the beginning his problem was to make sure that
em he made was an authentic poem; and in the world in which he lived,
could not quite fit poems into its scheme of things, his sense of himself
ed him the sole means for testing authenticity.

Whitman had always wanted more than this. Like Poe and Emerson,
s not altogether happy in his knowledge of the divisiveness for which
le as poet made him the speaker. Such knowledge made possible a
tion of man as being necessarily defined by man—simple, separate
His hope was always that, coming to know this much, he might come to
more. The momentum built up in the poetic act might be sufficient to
im who initiated it into such knowledge as would make for a transcen-
of divisiveness. To discover the simple and separate and to celebrate it
then necessarily be to define the democratic man en-masse. The dilem-
as inevitable, perhaps the product of the American poet's discovery that
ienation which was a condition of his writing his kind of poetry was too
to bear. Like Emerson and Poe, in the end Whitman wanted to be some-
of a "philosopher"; and he came to write poems in which integrating
ent is set against, not transformed by, sensibility and imagination.
ere is, for example, the cosmic inclusiveness of "Chanting the Square
," which by virtue of adding Satan to the Trinity intends to encompass
hole of man's spiritual experience. But just how much is this intention
ed? For the definition of each of the Persons of this Square is charged
he regular Whitmanian assertion of self. It is said of Christ, for example:

All sorrow, labor, suffering, I, tallying it, absorb in myself,
Many times have I been rejected, taunted, put in prison, and
   crucified, and many times shall be again,
All the world have I given up for my dear brothers' and
   sisters' sake, for the soul's sake . . .

an make us believe in no one but Whitman and in nothing else but his
s poet-spider—in the words already quoted, launching "forth filament,
nt, filament out of itself. . . . " It is not as a Holy Ghost but as a
man, located squarely in nineteenth-century America, that he can, as he
t the end of the poem, "Breathe my breath also through these songs."
hanting the Square Deific," then, fails as "The Sleepers" does not, because
tention is too explicitly "philosophical" and abstract and its movement
rticulation not sufficiently under the control of its maker. Its ideas are

ego is shown celebrating its oneness with all other egos. In the night, in sleep, the poet is able to lose his sense of individuated self and make vital contact with all other selves. Yet in the poem there emerges a sense of creativity so strong as to argue against the very oneness which is the poet's intended subject.

The poem begins thus:

I wander all night in my vision,
   Stepping with light feet, swiftly and noiselessly stepping and
      stopping,
   Bending with open eyes over the shut eyes of sleepers,
   Wandering and confused, lost to myself, ill-assorted, con-
      tradictory,
   Pausing, gazing, bending, and stopping.

"My vision" is the key phrase here. For as the poem develops, the night is conceived of as the poet's lover, rendering him utterly passive. In this state he envisions himself as possessing and possessed by all men and all women, good and evil, now so undifferentiated as to be universally beautiful. He comes to see that it is "the night and sleep (which have) liken'd them and restored them." The night then is given its richest definition:

I too pass from the night,
   I stay a while away O night, but I return to you again and
      love you.

Why should I be afraid to trust myself to you?
   I am not afraid, I have been well brought forward by you,

I love the rich running day, but I do not desert her in whom
      I lay so long,
   I know not how I came of you and I know not where I go
      with you, but I know I came well and shall go well.

I will stop only a time with the night, and rise betimes,
   I will duly pass the day O my mother, and duly return to you.

It is thus a primal source of creativity, lover and genetrix, to which the poet must return, even as he must leave it for his daytime life. Most important, it is a source within the poet, the deepest aspect of himself as authentic person. Returning to his mother, he returns to himself as dreamer-creator, returns to the act with which the poem begins; for it is he who has "liken'd . . . and . . . restored" all to beauty.

The passage is often read as involving a notion of the transcendental source of being, so that "night" equals death-in-life and life-in-death, dissolution of the temporal into the eternal, and the like. Yet the form of the poem, its movement from the picture of the envisioning poet to a series of catalogues and narratives of what he envisions, to the discovery that the act of envisioning makes all beautiful, then finally to the realization of the source of envisioning power—all this demonstrates a Whitman sufficiently conscious of his own commitment to isolated, egocentric creativity to manifest it even as he tries to transcend it. Lacking a hard-headed respect for the "other," he is more Emersonian than Emerson. If the soul is always beautiful, it is so because Whitman can envision it and thereby make it so, as he yields to the night-time power of his genius. For us, the poem is the act of the envisioning. The account of the source of the vision, its meaning and rationale, is part of that act and derives its power from the actor, not from the transcendental, pantheistic world-view toward which he seems to aspire. Whereas in "The Sleepers" Whitman argues for a transcendent One which would per se universalize the ego, he expresses the act of the ego striving to universalize itself by recreating the world in its own image. The poet here is the one who elsewhere wrote of the "noiseless patient spider" which, "to explore the vacant vast surrounding," has "launched forth filament, filament, filament out of itself. . . . "

Discovering and confirming his relationship to the world, the poet discovers the possibility that the nominally anti-poetic can be made into poetry itself. But if he thereby transforms the world, he does not thereby unify it. He gives the world a new meaning—transforming it by alienating it from itself and the crude workaday, anti-poetic reality which characterizes it. Doing so, he intensifies his own alienation. Doing so, however, he all the more intensifies his sense of himself as simple, separate, and creating—autonomous. He would create other persons like himself—in effect save them from that anti-poetic world to which the demands of their workaday life commit them, even as their workaday productions create it.

Meanness, ugliness, vice—*obviously* anti-poetic since they militate against the creativity which is at the heart of the poetic—all these the poet can appropriate by at once naming and loving them. He finds himself to be one event in a cosmic process and is thereby able to envisage the possibility of both the end and the beginning of the process. He would celebrate abundance, plenitude, and movement—growth. But at his best he does not lose himself in what he celebrates; his technique, his conception of poetry, the way his poems work, will not let him do so. He may have looked to a sort of Hegelian Absolute; he may well have felt that he was achieving it. Yet his poems show that he could not; he was compulsively a person, a single person.

Sometimes, as in "Out of the Cradle Endlessly Rocking," he establishes his relation to cosmic process by developing in an argument a series of carefully defined, clearly symbolic, ego-centered relationships. In "Out of the Cradle . . .," the adult makes a poem which is his means to understanding a childhood experience. The firm control in the poem (it is extraordinary here, especially for Whitman, but nonetheless it is not always a sign of the highest achievement of his poetry) is managed through the manipulation of this double point-of-view. Initially we are told of the range of experiences out of which this poem comes: the song of the bird, the place, the time, the memory

of the dead brother, and the as yet unnamed " cious than any" which gathers unto itself the m introductory overview. Then we are presented v loss of the beloved, and the song sung to object it bearable. Always we are aware that the poet-a the poem, seeks the "word stronger and more means finally to understand his reminiscences.

The points of view of child and adult are ke which reads:

> Demon or bird! (said the boy's soul,)
> Is it indeed toward your mate you sing
> For I, that was a child, my tongue's use
>   heard you,
> Now in a moment I know what I am f
> And already a thousand singers, a thous
>   louder and more sorrowful than yours,
> A thousand warbling echoes have starte
>   never to die.

Here the points of view are hypnotically merged discovers a child's potentiality for adult knowl potentiality, he can work toward its realization, follow automatically from the other. He asks for superior to all," which will once and for all pr willed himself to create. And it comes as he re manifesting the rhythm of life and death itself,

> Delaying not, hurrying not,
> Whisper'd me through the night, and
>   daybreak,
> Lisp'd to me the low and delicious wo
> And again death, death, death, death .

The merging of the points of view occurs as not and adult, but subject and object (i.e., "The sea me") are fused. The poet now knows the word, situation in which he can control its use, having fi boy and man, and having then fused the two phas end of the poem is to understand cosmic proces beloved through death and a consequent gain of a and death-in-life—if this is the end of the poem, no through a creative act, an assertion of life in the fa of the very person, the poet, whom death would d in life.

"Out of the Cradle . . . " is typical of those po

most
chief
is one
points
a part
creati
less n
which
make
any p
which
furnis

Ye
he wa
his re
conce
man.
know
take
dence
would
ma w
the al
great
thing
argur

Th
Deifi
the w
achiev
with

This
role
filam
Whi
says
"C
its in
and

not sufficiently Whitman's. This is also true of "Passage to India," wherein the ego at times loses sight and control of itself and celebrates a world it never made. Quite likely Whitman wanted it this way, as Poe wanted to move toward *Eureka*. Their faith would appear to have been that they had finally to lose themselves in the cosmos, so that they might be found. At this point they could neither yield themselves entirely nor ask that the world yield to them. They were asking more from poetry than it could give: absolution for their having been poets. The result was indifferent poetry, confused religion, and bad philosophy—a sign that they had gone beyond the outer limits of their basic style, which marked the outer limits of their power as selves.

A sense of such limits saved Whitman from the sort of grandiose mysticism for which he so often yearned and also from the excess of the "Personalism" which he as often preached. That he was, in spite of his wide-ranging reading, cut off from large areas of knowledge and large forms of discipline (subsumable under some such words as "orthodoxy" and "tradition") is obvious enough. This is a weakness not only complementary but necessary to the strength of his poems. His conception of poetry not only made for his poems; it also protected him from the world to which he addressed them. For it demanded that the anti-poetic world be at the most translatable into, at the least congruent with, the concept of self, or have no claim to reality at all. This is to a degree a mutilating conception of reality. Yet it is at the same time a source of strength, for Whitman perhaps *the* source of strength. The lesson is by now an old one: the miracle of the achieved poetic act is that by imaginative transformation it can derive its characteristic strength from the characteristic weakness of the culture in which it is performed.[3]

From *The Continuity of American Poetry* (Princeton: Princeton Univ. Press, 1961), pp. 57-58, 164-74.

---

3. I have throughout cited poems as Whitman finally revised them. It is worth noting, however, as Roger Asselineau in particular points out (in his *L'Evolution de Walt Whitman*), that the revisions are almost always in the direction of formal clarity and intellectual systematization; as a result many of the poems, as finally revised, have lost a certain vigor and fresh, primal quality. The earlier versions (particularly those in the 1860 *Leaves of Grass*) of many of the poems, I would add, are often more clearly poems in what I have termed the basic style than are the later ones, precisely because the earlier versions tend not to have the sort of "intellectualization" which cuts them off, relatively, from the basic style. (I have considered in detail the 1860 edition of *Leaves of Grass* in my Introduction to a facsimile reprint of it [Ithaca, 1961]. It is, I think, Whitman's greatest book.) Nonetheless, we must look always to the latest versions of the poems, in order fully to comprehend the final relationship of the poems to the basic style.

LOUIS L. MARTZ

Whitman and Dickinson

EXCEPT FOR a shared inheritance of Emersonian thought, which they put to quite different uses, Walt Whitman and Emily Dickinson have very little in common, whether in their personal lives or in their poetical manner. One thinks of the portrait of Walt in the first edition of *Leaves of Grass:* open-shirted, slouching, "one of the roughs"; Walt the printer, reporter, and newspaper editor, Walt the traveler to New Orleans and the Great Lakes, Walt the hospital attendant, moving among the wounded soldiers of the Civil War. And then one thinks of Emily, spending nearly all her days in Amherst, spending indeed the last twenty years of her life almost entirely within the confines of her father's yard, dressed in white, and sending forth her "letter to the World/ That never wrote to Me." We think of the long, loping, irregular lines of Whitman, his endless catalogues, his boundless inclusiveness:

> A Kentuckian walking the vale of the Elkhorn in my deer-skin
>   leggings, a Louisianian or Georgian,
> A boatman over lakes or bays or along coasts, a Hoosier,
>   Badger, Buckeye;
> At home on Kanadian snow-shoes or up in the bush, or with
>   fishermen off Newfoundland,
> At home in the fleet of ice-boats, sailing with the rest and
>   tacking,
> At home on the hills of Vermont or in the woods of Maine,
>   or the Texan ranch . . .
> A farmer, mechanic, artist, gentleman, sailor, quaker,
> Prisoner, fancy-man, rowdy, lawyer, physician, priest.[1]

And we think of Emily's clipped and rigorous selectivity:

> The Soul selects her own Society—
> Then—shuts the Door—
> To her divine Majority—
> Present no more—

.   .   .   .   .

1. With a few exceptions my quotations from Whitman are taken from the text of 1891-2 as presented in *The Collected Writings of Walt Whitman: Leaves of Grass*, Comprehensive Reader's Edition, ed. Harold W. Blodgett and Sculley Bradley (New York University Press, 1965).

I've known her—from an ample nation—
Choose One—
Then—close the Valves of her attention—
Like Stone—

These are the representations of two utterly different modes of poetry, each in its own way trying to find an answer to the problems of a world and a self hovering between dissolution and creation. Indeed, the external struggle of the Civil War and the internal struggle of the poets might be said to have their roots in much the same issue: a turbulent originality of purpose, unable any longer to accept the traditional modes of life and thought, struggling to create a new world: "The Modern Man I sing."

Surely no one was ever more thoroughly aware of his originality than Walt Whitman: he throws away the stanzas and the rhymes of traditional poetry; he refuses even to use the customary names of the months, calling them, in Biblical, Quaker fashion, Third-month or Fifth Month: the national holiday becomes "the fourth of Seventh-month." He insists on bringing into poetry materials hardly regarded as "poetic" in his day: the butcher-boy in his killing-clothes, the bus driver "with his interrogating thumb," the clam-digger tucking in his trouser-ends, the fare-collector going through the train, giving notice "by the jingling of loose change," picnics, and jigs, and a game of baseball, triphammers, fire-engines, stevedores, and sign-painters. He uses colloquial, archaic, or invented language unknown to the poetry of his time: "the blab of the pave," "my gore dribs," "rock me in billowy drowse," "flatting the flesh of my nose," the "limpsy" slave, "to dicker," "shoulder your duds," and "rest the chuff of your hand on my hip." It is all, as he proudly says, part of "my gab" and "my barbaric yawp."

Yet with all his exuberant originality, Whitman, like every poet, has his ancestors. We may feel them present in the long, rhythmic, flowing, unrhymed verses, in the parallel phrasing, in the frequent linking of lines by *and:*

And I know that the hand of God is the promise of my own,
And I know that the spirit of God is the brother of my own,
And that all the men ever born are also my brothers, and the
women my sisters and lovers. . . .

I am the poet of the Body and I am the poet of the Soul,
The pleasures of heaven are with me and the pains of hell are with
me,
The first I graft and increase upon myself, the latter I translate into
a new tongue.

Whether in manner or in substance, there seems to be only one essential precedent for such writing—the prophetic poetry of the Bible, particularly the prophetic books of the Old Testament, which Whitman knew thoroughly.

There has been of late a considerable tendency to deny the validity of the term "prophetic poetry" to Whitman's best work, although Whitman himself clearly aligned his poetry with this kind of writing. Thus in *Democratic Vistas* (1871) he proclaimed the need for a "prophetic literature of these States" and warned his countrymen: "If you would have greatness, know that you must conquer it through ages, centuries—must pay for it with a proportionate price. For you too, as for all lands, the struggle, the traitor, the wily person in office, scrofulous wealth, the surfeit of prosperity, the demonism of greed, the hell of passion, the decay of faith, the long postponement, the fossil-like lethargy, the ceaseless need of revolutions, prophets, thunderstorms, deaths, births, new projections and invigorations of ideas and men." [2] It has been argued that Whitman's conception of himself as a prophet was indeed the downfall of his poetry, as he came more and more to develop what he calls humorously, in "Song of Myself," "my prophetical screams." That is—so the charge runs—his tendency to make abstract assertions about the future grew, until he weakened his essential poetical power, his ability to deal concretely and dynamically with the world about him.

No doubt these charges against Whitman are true, except for some of the Civil War poems. I share the preference of many critics for the early editions of 1855 or 1860, as against the many revisions, rearrangements, and additions that Whitman made up to the time of his death in 1892. It is dangerous for a poet to allow himself to say, as Whitman says in one of the later poems ("Shut Not Your Doors"): "The words of my book nothing, the drift of it every thing," for a poet to whom words have become nothing does indeed run the risk that Whitman humorously prophesies in "Song of Myself," when he cries, "My ties and ballasts leave me." His "flights of a fluid and swallowing soul" may fly out too often beyond the human horizon, into a place where the air is too thin for poetry. But all this has nothing to do with the question of whether Whitman's poetry at its best deserves to be called *prophetic*.

To grasp Whitman's essential relation to the Biblical Prophets, we must keep in mind the original meaning of the word "prophet." For the prophet was not simply one who foretold the future; he was, in the old Greek meaning of the word, one who speaks for another—specifically, one who speaks for God and interprets the divine will to man. Thus we have the refrain of Ezekiel, "And the word of the Lord came unto me, saying . . . " Or in Jeremiah and Isaiah— "Thus saith the Lord." When the Hebrew prophets interpret the future, it is for the purpose of arousing their people to the needs and demands of the present, it is to exhort and warn their people that they must fulfill their faith now, be constant to their trust now, be true now to their appointed part in the divine mission. To convey that urgent, immediate sense of mission, the prophet's imagination reaches forth over the whole known world, comprehending in detail the life of the time in vast visions of creation and destruction, as in Ezekiel's great vision of the doomed wealth and power of Tyre:

    2. *The Collected Writings of Walt Whitman: Prose Works* 1892, ed. Floyd Stovall (2 vols., New York University Press, 1963-4), II, 416, 423.

Tarshish was thy merchant by reason of the multitude of all kind
of riches; with silver, iron, tin, and lead, they traded in thy
fairs.
Javan, Tubal, and Meshech, they were thy merchants: they traded
the persons of men and vessels of brass in thy market.
They of the house of Togarmah traded in thy fairs with horses and
horsemen and mules.
The men of Dedan were thy merchants; many isles were the merchandise of thine hand: they brought thee for a present horns
of ivory and ebony.
Syria was thy merchant by reason of the multitude of the wares of
thy making: they occupied in thy fairs with emeralds, purple,
and broidered work, and fine linen, and coral, and agate.
Judah, and the land of Israel, they were thy merchants: they traded
in thy market wheat of Minnith, and Pannag, and honey, and
oil, and balm.
Damascus was thy merchant in the multitude of the wares of thy
making, for the multitude of all riches; in the wine of Helbon,
and white wool.
Dan also and Javan going to and fro occupied in thy fairs: bright
iron, cassia, and calamus, were in thy market.

*   *   *   *   *

Haran, and Canneh, and Eden, the merchants of Sheba, Asshur,
and Chilmad, were thy merchants.
These were thy merchants in all sorts of things, in blue clothes, and
broidered work, and in chests of rich apparel, bound with
cords, and made of cedar, among thy merchandise.

We need look no farther than this to find the prime precedent for
Whitman's enormous catalogues: it is the essence of the prophet to comprehend the whole of the living earth within his view. But if Whitman is in this
way a kind of prophet, for whom does he prophesy, for whom does he speak?
"I celebrate myself, and sing myself," he declares in the opening bravado of
his major poem. But what is this self? It is a something made up of "the
thoughts of all men in all ages"; it is like "the grass that grows wherever the
land is and the water is"; its "intricate purpose" is one with that of the
"Fourth-month showers" and the "mica on the side of a rock." It is a universal
sympathy, a universal consciousness, absorbing all into itself, becoming one
with all and all with one:

Through me many long dumb voices,
Voices of the interminable generations of prisoners and slaves,
Voices of the diseas'd and despairing and of thieves and dwarfs . . .

When he listens he hears "all sounds running together, combined, fused or

following"; when he touches he has "instant conductors all over me whether
I pass or stop,/ They seize every object and lead it harmlessly through me."
As he says, smiling at the extravagance, nothing, nothing can evade him:

> In vain the mastodon retreats beneath its own powder'd bones,
> In vain objects stand leagues off and assume manifold shapes,
> In vain the ocean settling in hollows and the great monsters lying
>   low,
> In vain the buzzard houses herself with the sky,
> In vain the snake slides through the creepers and logs,
> In vain the elk takes to the inner passes of the woods,
> In vain the razor-bill'd auk sails far north to Labrador,
> I follow quickly, I ascend to the nest in the fissure of the cliff.

Whatever happens, wherever it happens, "I am the man, I suffer'd, I was
there."

Thus, in his vast prophetic catalogues we find each animal, each man and
woman, caught in a characteristic occupation, vividly caught, and skillfully
arranged in a list that is far more than a random listing. For his aim, as he
says in "Proto-Leaf," 1860, is this:

> . . . I will show that there is no imperfection in male or female,
>   or in the earth, or in the present—and can be none in the
>   future,
> And I will show that whatever happens to anybody, it may be
>   turned to beautiful results—And I will show that nothing can
>   happen more beautiful than death;
> And I will thread a thread through my poems that no one thing in
>   the universe is inferior to another thing,
> And that all the things of the universe are perfect miracles, each as
>   profound as any.[3]

Hence, with a mild, leveling wit, we find Whitman placing the "elegant" and
the "common," the "important" and the "trivial" side by side, with the bland
assumption that all are of equal interest, equal value, whether it be the art-song
of the trained singer or the art-sound of the carpenter's tool:

> The pure contralto sings in the organ loft,
> The carpenter dresses his plank, the tongue of his foreplane whistles
>   its wild ascending lisp . . .
> The duck-shooter walks by silent and cautious stretches,
> The deacons are ordain'd with cross'd hands at the altar,
> The spinning girl retreats and advances to the hum of the big
>   wheel,

---

3. See *Leaves of Grass: Facsimile Edition of the 1860 Text*, with introduction by Roy Harvey Pearce
(Ithaca, N.Y., Cornell University Press, 1961).

The farmer stops by the bars as he walks on a First-day loafe and
looks at the oats and rye,
The lunatic is carried at last to the asylum a confirm'd case,
(He will never sleep any more as he did in the cot in his mother's
bed-room;)

Deacon and duck-shooter are equally reverent in their pursuits; spinning-girl
and farmer have equally creative tasks; and even the madman has someone—his
mother—for whom he has been an object of love and care.

The President holding a cabinet council is surrounded by the great
Secretaries,
On the piazza walk three matrons stately and friendly with twined
arms,
The crew of the fish-smack pack repeated layers of halibut in the
hold . . .

Cabinet council, twined matrons, packed layers of halibut thus come together
in a thoroughly democratic equivalence!
The self he sings is nothing less than the power of his human consciousness:
a divine power, enabling the prophet to "hear and behold God in every object,"
enabling him to say: "I find letters from God dropt in the street, and every
one is sign'd by God's name." Yet it is also a power resident, in some measure,
in every man: "It is you talking just as much as myself, I act as the tongue
of you,/Tied in your mouth, in mine it begins to be loosen'd." "The mere fact
consciousness," says Whitman, is an awesome miracle:

these forms, the power of motion,
The least insect or animal, the senses, eyesight, love,
The first step I say awed me and pleas'd me so much,
I have hardly gone and hardly wish'd to go any farther,
But stop and loiter all the time to sing it in ecstatic songs.

Verbal consciousness, fully developed, is enough, says Whitman, to assure us
of our divinity. It is a fact that he apprehends, in his own favorite terms, by
leaning, and loafing, and loitering, not by cogitation, not by analytic thinking.
Consciousness, for Whitman, arises by accepting and encouraging to the full
the miracles of "seeing, hearing, feeling." The universe for Whitman requires
no rational explanation, no analysis, no theology: it is enough to be "the
caresser of life wherever moving."
   Moving, to live consciously in the full flow of the divine, creative process—
this is the heart of Whitman's prophecy. Yet he is not a callow, easy optimist:
he knows the hounded slave, the massacre in Texas, the "hiss of the surgeon's
knife." Whitman is aware that the honest caresser of life must draw his fingers
across the jagged points and the gaping wounds; and in his later poems he
becomes ever more deeply aware of death, as in the conclusion of "Out of the

Cradle Endlessly Rocking." But the sense of death, the melancholy moments, the awareness of the "down-hearted doubters"—all these things are absorbed into and transcended by the outgoing and onsweeping wonder of consciousness, brought to the peak of creativity by the wonder of the human word. "The words of the true poems give you more than poems," he declares:

> Whom they take they take into space to behold the birth of stars,
>   to learn one of the meanings,
> To launch off with absolute faith, to sweep through the ceaseless
>   rings and never be quiet again.

From *The Poem of the Mind* (New York: Oxford Univ. Press, 1966), pp. 82-90.

MARTIN GREEN

Twain and Whitman

We shall presently be indifferent to being looked down upon by
a nation no bigger and no better than our own [England]. We
made the telegraph a practical thing; we invented the fast press,
the sewing machine, the sleeping and parlor car, the telephone,
the ironclad, we have done our share for the century, we have
introduced foretelling of the weather.

THIS COMES from Twain's Notebook. There is plenty of 'Americanism' in
Melville, Emerson, Hawthorne, but to find it basing itself on such unequivocal
materialism, you would have to go outside the ranks of the imaginative writers,
to someone like Andrew Carnegie—a friend of Twain's and patron of
Whitman's, incidentally. Or to some popular orator in the Frontier tradition.

They belonged to that tradition in the good ways, too, however. Both had,
for instance, a marked affinity with Lincoln. Whitman's feeling for the dead
President, and his self-identification with the national cult, is a part of his
literary product. But that feeling was more than sentimental and literary. His
description of an ideal President in 'The 18th Presidency!' in 1856, exactly fits
the figure Lincoln made of himself in 1860 and after. There was a genuine unity
between them. While Twain ('the Lincoln of our literature', as Howells called
him) inherited the lighter side of Lincoln's rôle as backwoods sage in polite
society, Twain and Lincoln are America's two supreme public figures in the
Frontier tradition of humour.* Lincoln found there his fund of fables and dirty
jokes, his skill in telling stories, his pose of naïveté, his conscious drawl, his
melancholy, his sudden savagery, his power of burlesque—he once mimicked
a political opponent so closely and savagely, in front of him and a crowd, in
every phrase and tone and gesture, that the man was reduced to public tears.
The affinity worked in the other direction, too. Lincoln read *Leaves of Grass*
one of the few who did—and was impressed—one of a still smaller number.
He died before Twain's work was known, but he was a great admirer of
Artemus Ward and Petroleum V. Nasby. These three, Lincoln, Whitman,
Twain, as statesman, prophet, entertainer, stand together and express the same
America, in a way hardly anyone else can equal. Emerson, Melville, Hawthorne,

---

* There are more links than an Englishman expects between that tradition and political life
in America; Twain was himself a kind of political oracle in his later years, as was Davy Crockett
before him, and Will Rogers after.

all spoke for and to a much more limited audience. Twain's and Whitman's admirers (Bernard de Voto, for instance) have of course stressed this Americanness, this non-literary quality, in their heroes; and scholarship about them still forms a separate current, a warm frothy Gulf Stream of positive thinking, in the critical ocean.

Then they had the gift, so rare among literary men, so necessary in public relations, for adopting in their own name the language of a group, a category; the group-language of the New York ferryboat men, the Broadway bus-drivers, the soldiers in hospital; or of the Nevada miners, the Mississippi river-pilots, the Connecticut businessmen; languages formed to express not the private self-definition of the speaker, but his public self-identification with the listeners. Whitman, for instance, was very successful in maintaining personal relationships on that level, with a good deal of emotion invested in them. He rather avoided relationships involving that other use of language, where narrowly defined meanings are dominant, and broadly unifying emotions are avoided. His personal style, in letters, is largely unformed. For him and for Twain, other people were a panorama of groups, types, trades, classes, rather than the dramas of self-discovery and self-salvation they were for—to take an extreme example—D. H. Lawrence, but also, in some degree, Emerson, Melville, Hawthorne.

Both were profoundly disorganised minds. They were strikingly incapable of organising a long piece of writing. They were incapable of a coherent attitude to a general topic, except where public opinion made that universal, as in the case of slavery after the war. They scarcely had coherent imaginative personalities. Twain's contradictory feelings about, for instance, Hannibal, and Whitman's about democracy, were not different aspects of a complexity, but unreconciled separate attitudes.

At the same time, no one presented to the world a more unified theatrical front. For all their seeming, and genuine, naïveté, they had highly sophisticated public personalities. They dressed to dramatise themselves; Twain in his white plantation-owner's suit, Whitman in his plebeian flannel shirt and broad-brimmed hat. They aimed at conspicuousness; Twain strolling down Fifth Avenue just as people came out of church on Sundays, Whitman writing from Boston, 'Of course I cannot walk through Washington Street (their Broadway here) without creating an immense sensation'. They wrote about themselves incessantly; not only in their major works, but for newspapers and magazines. They were interviewed, quoted, biographised, photographed (in the most arranged poses), painted, sculpted, sketched, more than any writers before them. Whitman wrote little articles about himself appearing anonymously or pseudonymously, describing his appearance and personality, and saying how much he was loved, and which shops had the best photographs of him for sale. And they played these rôles not only in their creative work and in newspaper interviews, but on at least two intermediate theatres; on the lecture platform and in private with disciples. We are accustomed to speak knowingly of the artist's mask nowadays, and to imply that it is part of every writer's normal apparatus; but what we find in Twain and Whitman reminds us how private, how discreet, most writers' gestures are. It is not to Yeats or Joyce we can compare their public personas, but to Wild Bill Hickock and Joaquin Miller. Their sense of a public, an enormous, faceless, undiscriminating public, had penetrated their private lives; their heights and depths of emotion related to moments involving them and an audience.

Reading Twain's accounts of his speech at the Grant dinner (the height of joy) or the one for Emerson, Whittier, and Holmes (the depths of despair) you might think this trait merely the result of his platform career, or of the talent that embodied. But Whitman, who had neither that career nor that talent, had the same temperament, the same radical showmanship. His love of public performance is at the heart of his poetic inspiration. During the crucial years before 1855 he rode up and down Broadway beside the drivers of buses, reciting at the top of his voice into the mid-town din; and, as he says, 'the influence of those Broadway omnibus jaunts and drivers and declamations and escapades undoubtedly entered into the gestation of *Leaves of Grass*'.

Lastly, perhaps most important for our present purposes, they were both easy liars. Whitman's accounts of himself, for both general and private consumption, were lavishly falsified; he wrote kind criticisms and bold defences of his own work under other people's names; he wrote, for instance, an introductory essay to his poems, and sent it to W. M. Rossetti, assuring him that it was by William O'Connor. Richard Chase says, 'At least he does not come bounding up to us with that doglike guilelessness our contemporary culture admires', but that does not soothe away our sense of protest. Quite apart from who these doglike contemporaries might be (a fine example of the defensive red herring), we surely see Whitman paying the artistic price of this habitual duplicity in, for instance, 'Children of Adam'. Not that a serious writer has to be literally truthful, but he has to have a higher opinion of his reader's ability to detect a lie, a subtler conception of what a lie is, a subtler conception of his whole relationship as a writer to his reader. Whitman's conception was too like that of an advertiser to his public—or of Davy Crockett to his constituents.

Among Twain's reminiscences, some have been identified as not only lavishly fictionalised, but as having happened to other people in the first place. And he pays the artistic price in, for instance, 'The Private History of a Campaign that Failed'; where we are left saying, 'But how *did* it feel? Why did you join, what did you think at the time, why did you lose faith?' It obviously wasn't just funny at the time; nor could the men involved have been *that* simplistically boyish; he has given us a palpably false account. The same is true of the duels he got involved in in Nevada; what was such an experience like? Not that he need give us the literal, or even the sober, truth. But in his fantasy we expect to find some evidence that such an event did in fact happen to him—that he was *capable* of such an experience—because if he wasn't the story is in the crucial sense a lie.

We tend nowadays to imply that there are no limits to the amount of fabrication and suppression a writer can employ in turning his experience into a book; but in fact literature is closely related to truth-telling of a certain sort. The central problem of the 'American' heritage—of that mass of rich legend and language taken over by the writers of mid-nineteenth-century America—

was its very different sense of the truth. There was a much broader sense of permissible gesture in all the great figures and legends of that tradition, and a much weaker interest in moral-psychological plausibility. There was a much louder, laxer, stagier relation between writer and reader. These gestures, these relationships, had produced the imaginative material the serious writers seized on, but they were at war with crucial literary criteria.

When Henry James was explaining why he had treated so little ' "unconventional" American life', he alleged the need to use the ugly local dialects, made ugly by a confusion between 'the speech of the soil and the speech of the newspaper'; however partial this antithesis, James certainly symbolises that faculty in the literary conscience which was thereby alienated from the 'American' material. It is because Twain and Whitman had so little of that faculty, had so odd a form of that conscience, that we are at so much of a loss when we read them nowadays.

Different as they are, we feel, if we read them honestly, that both are equally non-literary. This feeling takes the form, when we read Whitman, of anguished protests—'You're making a fool of yourself—look what you're saying—this is exactly what you can't *do* in a poem'. In Twain's case, until we dismiss our literary expectations, it takes the form of a resentful impatience, 'Don't be so funny—don't be so charming—what did you really feel?'

Non-literary here refers of course to the major meanings of literary. Obviously Twain was one of the world's great artists in the minor meanings. Nobody ever used words more skilfully; he defined and achieved his purposes beautifully. But in the use of language to aesthetic effects, the most important surely involve the definition of truths of personal experience—personal here implying a self-responsible adult personality, whose reactions and discriminations are in some measure moral self-commitments, whose self-expression seeks the response of other such personalities. It is in this sense that Twain is not concerned with personal truth, and that therefore literary criteria do not apply themselves to his work. They do apply themselves to Whitman—because he so loudly offers to discuss personal truth—but they are hideously offended by what they find there. He is non-literary in the minor meanings of the word, too.

In Whitman's case the point is fairly easily made. The 'I' of 'Song of Myself' is first of all Walt Whitman, later all Americans, later the Unconscious or World Spirit; and though there is some humorous interplay of differentness between those selves, there is also a more remarkable indeterminate sliding from one into another. The self-responsible personality disappears. The crucial distinction, between what the poet felt, and what he might have felt if he had been somebody else, is fatally blurred; and this blurring extends to his tone as well as to his vision. He is not speaking *to* any more than *as* a person. The social situation he sets up with his readers is always tending to become that of a speaker before a huge shapeless crowd, highly excitable and responsive and uncritical, each of whom he has to merge with himself, and with each other. There are no satisfactory persons in Whitman's poetic world, nei-

ther the 'I' nor the 'You', and consequently there is no satisfaction in it for
the reader.

Despite Whitman's official reputation, many literary people will grant this
argument fairly easily. The difficulty is to make the opposite point, that
Whitman remains an important writer.

This is not just because of the fragments of successful poetry that are
scattered through *Leaves of Grass*. Richard Chase has put the case for them very
ably in *Walt Whitman Reconsidered;* one would add only that Whitman is also,
from time to time, a very poignant poet of sexual provocation.

> 'Ever the old inexplicable query, ever that thorn'd thumb, that
>   breath of itches and thirsts,
> Ever the vexer's hoot, hoot, till we find where the sly one hides
>   and bring him forth,
> Ever love, ever the sobbing liquid of life,
> Ever the bandage under the chin, ever the trestle of death.'

And in another piece, after a reference to the 'guile, anger, lust, hot wishes I
dared not speak', he continues,

> 'Was called by my nighest name by clear loud voices of young
>   men, as they saw me approaching or passing,
> Felt their arms on my neck as I stood, or the negligent leaning of
>   their flesh against me as I sat,
> Saw many I loved in the street or ferry-boat or public assembly,
>   yet never told them a word,
> Lived the same life with the rest, the same laughing, gnawing,
>   sleeping,
> Play'd the part that still looks back on the actor or actress,
> The same old role, the role that is what we make it, as great as
>   we like,
> Or as small as we like, or both great and small.'

There are . . . moments of graphic sexual description in his poetry, but
they are always succeeded, or interfused, with something so much the opposite that it remains an essentially painful experience to read *Leaves of Grass*
with one's literary sensibility aroused. ('I dote on myself, there is that lot of
me and all so luscious' may serve as a sufficient reminder of all that is referred to.) Whitman is not only non-literary, he is anti-literary. He offers to
discuss personal experience, and then forces on us everything but that—catalogues of objects, political exhortations, ideas of sexuality, day-dreams, grotesque posturings. Even his catalogues are of things he had read about, not
seen and heard himself. In a word, he does not tell us the truth. Quite often,
he tells lies; he says he has felt and seen things which he has not. Again and
again, he makes a fool of himself; having invited us into his mind, with our
keenest expectations aroused, he appears before us in a tatty series of road

company spangles, cutting capers he's never properly practised. And all the time he asks his readers to cease to be persons (people who respect their own emotions, who commit themselves in a reaction only when that further extends and defines their personality in new and risky areas of experience) and to become partisans, members of a crowd, merging with each other in a stock response. In reading Whitman, therefore, despite moments of pleasure, a reader has to force himself, to go against his nature as reader.

In *not* reading Whitman, however, an intelligent man also makes an unnatural sacrifice. Not for the fragments of successful poetry, but for the outline of a significant literary venture that everywhere comes through when you read sympathetically. Whitman confronted the ideas of his time, some of its crucial experience, its poetic theory, its language, and strove to make something large out of them. He failed atrociously in nine-tenths of his particular effects, but his general intention, coming dimly through, engages our interest. One can understand why he was a source for better poets, and very different ones, coming after him. But we can only respond to that intention, act on that interest, if we switch off the spotlight of critical awareness—the crucial component in any literary discipline—and work in the penumbra of a general humanism; a general interest in intellectual history, aesthetic theory and so on. It is because it is so hard for literary critics to do this, and because Whitman must, as time goes by, become more and more their property, that he is generally neglected today. With rare exceptions like Mr Chase, he has been abandoned to the obscurity of an official reputation; and so long as literary study retains its rigour, this is perhaps the kindest fate that can befall him, unjust though it is. The solution to the problem of 'American' literature has in his case been oblivion.

From *Re-Appraisals: Some Commonsense Readings in American Literature* (1965; rpt. New York: Norton, 1967), pp.113-43.

ROGER ASSELINEAU

Conclusion

THIS DOUBLE study of Whitman the man and of Whitman the poet during the forty-odd years during which *Leaves of Grass* germinated and grew reveals that he increasingly understood and used the potentialities present in him from the beginning of his poetic career. Whitman realized it himself in 1888:

> . . . I set out with the intention also of indicating or hinting
> some point-characteristics which I since see (though I did not
> then, at least not definitely) were bases and object-urgings toward
> those "Leaves" from the first.

The ideas and the main themes were indeed gradually brought out and clarified. The Protean poet of 1855 who metamorphosed in turn into everything that lived, rejoiced, and suffered, was succeeded as early as 1860 by the less prolix "chanter of pains and joys, uniter of here and hereafter." The sensual and disconnected mystical intuitions of the first edition led ten years later to the geometric theology of "Chanting the Square Deific" which interpreted and systematized his insights without changing their essential nature or warping their meaning. In the course of successive editions, *Leaves of Grass* was subjected to a gradual intellectualization which made the sense and the purpose of the book more accessible by introducing order and logic into the chaos of the original poems.

But this rationalization presented dangers which Whitman did not completely avoid. For, by insisting more and more on the intellectual content of his mystic revelations, he ran the risk of losing contact with the living reality of the physical world and of insensibly giving the first place to lifeless abstractions. As a matter of fact, we have had occasion to notice the increasingly abstract character of his poetic language. But one should not overemphasize this aspect of his evolution, as Malcolm Cowley, for instance, did. "When Lilacs Last in the Dooryard Bloom'd" is far from being as conventional as he would have it, and it must not be forgotten on the other hand that *Specimen Days* which was composed between 1876 and 1881, offers the same wealth of concrete details and sensuous data as the first editions of *Leaves of Grass*. Whatever may be said, Whitman never completely lost his hold on the real. Despite his increasing care for order and clarity he never fell into that other form of dryness which is dogmatism. In a poem of 1891, near the end of his

life, he still evoked the impenetrable mystery of the world, whose secret neither
he nor anyone else has ever been able to pierce:

> In every object, mountain, tree, and star—in every
> birth and life,
> As part of each—evolv'd from each—meaning, behind the ostent,
> A mystic cipher waits infolded.

While these changes were taking place, Whitman gave in gradually to the
"resistless gravitation of Spiritual Law," and gave increasing emphasis to the
spirit, the soul, in preference to matter, to God rather than the Creation, to
death rather than life, to the future rather than the present. Newton Arvin,
being a materialist himself, has strongly reproached Whitman for that tendency
toward spiritualism which, according to him, involves a diminution of lucidity
and a loss of intellectual vigor. But the problem is not quite so simple, for
Whitman never chose between materialism and spiritualism. His poems of
1855 are already spiritualistic insofar as he interprets his mystic illuminations,
and his last writings are still materialistic insofar as they reveal an unchanged
attachment to the physical world. He was indeed perfectly aware both of that
shift of emphasis and of the permanence of that duality:

> In youth and maturity Poems are charged with sunshine and
> varied pomp of day; but as the soul more and more takes prece-
> dence, (the sensuous still included,) the Dusk becomes the poet's
> atmosphere. I too have sought, and ever seek, the brilliant sun,
> and make my songs according. But as I grow old, the half-lights
> of evening are far more to me.

This victory of the soul was won through the decline of his body. With
age and illness, his sensual ardors and, consequently, his mysticism calmed
down, and his inspiration became proportionally poorer. The spring gradually
dried up. In his old age, the powerful glow of his poetry was reduced to a thin
trickle. The last forceful poems that he wrote date from 1871. In 1876 he could
add only twenty-one new poems to his book and they were very short at that.
There was even one among that number which was not original; its subject
was borrowed from Michelet. In 1881, there were only nineteen new poems,
and not one of them was longer than one page. Besides, he often evinced, as
in "My Picture Gallery," more ingenuity than power. But he nonetheless
persisted in writing poetry up to the end and composed two more collections
of poems before his death, *November Boughs* and *Good-Bye My Fancy,* in which,
unfortunately, he could only repeat weakly what he had formerly proclaimed
in a stentorian voice. He was even obliged, in order to fill out his thin volumes,
to resort to prose texts and to old material he had originally rejected. He had
reached such a stage of decadence that whereas in the years 1855 to 1860 the
"leaves of grass" were flourishing and he gathered them profusely, he now had
nothing more to offer than a few "lingering sparse leaves."

This loss of force, however, was compensated for by an undeniable progress in form. The disordered impetuosity of the first editions was by degrees disciplined and brought under control. After the Civil War, the chaotic, anarchistic poems were succeeded by well-constructed poems in which the various themes were skillfully intertwined and the reader was guided by repetitions and burdens. The style was more polished, too, and the words chosen with greater care. The successive revisions reveal an increasingly surer taste and a sense of finish which Whitman had lacked completely at the beginning. Negligences of style, improprieties, grammatical errors were thus gradually eliminated. And, at the same time, the rhythm became less loose and more regular. The music, at first neglected, little by little gained in prestige and importance. Imperceptibly, by slow degrees, the inspired mystic of 1855 became more and more involved in problems of form and expression and was eventually metamorphosed into an artist.

Does that mean that Whitman made these concessions in order to reach a larger public? It does not seem so. We have seen the reproaches which were heaped upon him with each new publication of his book. They had practically no influence on him. True, he suppressed here and there, as far as content goes, a few sexual images which were too bold and needlessly gross, but he nonetheless maintained until the end the crudest poems of "Calamus" and "Children of Adam." As to form, he did his best to make his instrument emit more harmonious sounds, but he always refused to go back to regular verse and, until his death, he used the free verse which he had himself created.

The life and career of Whitman thus present a remarkable continuity. During the forty years which he dedicated to *Leaves of Grass* he made no major change in his philosophy. The same spirit which had impelled him in 1855 carried him until his death in the same direction—though, it is true, with less and less force. His thought, like his technique, remained fundamentally the same. His life shows a rupture, but it took place between 1850 and 1855, when he abruptly decided to break with his past and devote himself to his great work. "Make the Works," he suddenly resolved one day, a decision which recalls that of Montaigne to withdraw into his "librairie" and turn his back on the world. From then on his evolution continued evenly and his work gives the impression of a gradual maturation and steady enrichment, of a slow and deepening apprehension of certain truths of which he had had an intuition from the beginning. Although it would be a very artificial game, one could almost deduce a posteriori the last poems from the very first. At any rate, it is easy to understand why he never felt the need to divide his poems into several collections. In proportion as they were born, they became integral to the pre-existent ensemble. From this process grew this single book, the work of a whole life.

Despite its unity, *Leaves of Grass* has, of course, neither the rigor nor the cohesion of a philosophical system. It is a bundle of contradictory tendencies, a sum of themes and ideas which are, to some extent, incompatible. Whitman hesitated between matter and spirit, love of life and the attraction of death, liberty, and authority, the individual and the masses. As a matter of fact, he

never intended to build up a philosophy. "I will not be a great philospher,"
he declared even before beginning his work, and he knew that his book was
full of contradictions and paradoxes. As he grew older, he tried to put more
order and clarity in this thought, but the original inner tensions subsisted until
the end. This did not displease him, however. His work thus encompassed all
systems and enabled each reader to remain himself. And, after all, in so doing,
he merely followed the example of his master Emerson and illustrated in his
own way the principle of "negative capability" formulated by Keats.

This long fidelity of Whitman to himself and to his contradictions is neither
stagnation nor immobility. On the contrary, it is the result of a relentless battle.
It is not by chance that he loved the adjective "agonistic"; he fully deserves
himself the epithet "agonistes," which Milton applied to Samson. He is the
poet of optimism and of joy, but all his life he had to struggle with despair—
despair which was caused by his contemporaries who were so often unworthy
of living in a democracy, despair which was caused by his own condition, too.
He had dreamed, as he wrote in one of his notebooks, of becoming "an old
man whose life has been magnificently developed," full of "faith in whatever
happens" "strong and wise and beautiful at 100 years old" like Merlin, but,
at fifty-four, he was struck by a paralytic attack and forced to lead after his
sixtieth year a life which became more and more sedentary and dull. He did
not give in, however, and all those who knew him in his old age have done
homage to his courage:

> During these long years of suffering no one has ever heard
> him utter a word of complaint . . . Every moment of his life
> tallied with the teachings of his books, [wrote T. B. Harned].

And in 1890 Robert Ingersoll lyrically proclaimed:

> He has not been soured by slander or petrified by prejudice;
> neither calumny nor flattery has made him revengeful or arrogant.
> Now sitting by the fireside, in the winter of life,
>   His jocund heart still beating in his breast,
> he is just as brave, and calm and kind as in manhood's proudest
> days, when roses blossomed in his cheeks.

Indeed, he succeeded in eliminating from his last poems all traces of rancor
or physical pain, striving "to keep up yet the lilt" in spite of his "snowy hairs,"
to sing "with gay heart" and a "blithe throat," like a "true conqueror" of life.

Under his apparent indolence, this voluptuous loafer had thus a core of
strength and a powerful will which no trial could curb, which illness, old age,
and failure were equally unable to break. This sensual poet was also a stoic,
a disciple of Epictetus, from whose *Enchiridion* he had chosen a quotation
which he used as a letter-head in his last years: "a little spark of soul dragging
a great lummux [sic] of a corpse-body clumsily to and fro around." This "little

spark of soul" effectively animated to the end his great half-paralyzed body and until the last moment inspired his poems.

The most difficult battle, however, was not with illness, but with his wild homosexual desires, which never left him at peace and constantly menaced his balance. All who saw him admired his serenity and his perfect moral health; no one suspected the torments which lacerated him. It was probably his art which saved him by permitting him to express (in the etymological meaning of the word) the turbulent passions which obsessed him. Poetry was for him a means of purification which, if it did not make him normal, at least permitted him to retain his balance in spite of his anomaly. In this sense, as we have tried to show, his *Leaves of Grass* are "fleurs du mal," "flowers of evil." His poetry is not the song of a demigod or a superman, as some of his admirers would have it, but the sad chant of a sick soul seeking passionately to understand and to save itself. He was thinking of himself, perhaps, when he wrote these lines about the actor, Junius Brutus Booth:

> He illustrated Plato's rule that to the forming of an artist of
> the very highest rank a dash of insanity, or what the world calls
> insanity, is indispensable.

His anomaly, which in all likelihood was what drove him to write *Leaves of Grass,* also explains certain of his limitations, and notably his inability to renew himself as he grew older—unlike Goethe. He lived too much alone, too much wrapped up in himself. Nothing ever came to change the image of the world which he had made for himself between 1850 and 1855. He spent all his life in the solitude of his inner universe, "solitary, singing in the West." But his isolation weighed upon him (hence his compensatory dreams of democratic brotherhood), and it even drove him to despair sometimes. Hence the cries of suffering which escaped him and which often interrupt his hymn to life. As Federico Garcia Lorca, who knew the same torments, so well understood, he is, despite appearances, the poet of anguish. Whitman, struck by its sadness, even copied this passage from one of Dickens' letters, he probably thought it applied very well to his own case:

> Why is it that, as with poor David, a sense comes always crush-
> ing on me now, when I fall into low spirits, as of one happiness
> I have missed in life, and one friend and companion I have never
> made?

Whitman had thus, at the very core of himself, a sense of defeat and frustration. He had had the ambition to create two masterpieces: a book of immortal poems and a life, the nobility and greatness of which would become legendary. He succeeded in one respect only, but his failure was, perhaps, the condition of that success.

From *The Evolution of Walt Whitman: The Creation of a Book* (Cambridge: The Belknap Press of the Harvard Univ. Press, 1962), pp. 253-60. Footnotes have been suppressed.

SELECTED BIBLIOGRAPHY

Editions

Allen, G. W., and Sculley Bradley, eds. *The Collected Writings of Walt Whitman*. New York: New York Univ. Press, 1961- . A CEAA edition.

Blodgett, Harold W., and Sculley Bradley, eds. *Leaves of Grass: Comprehensive Readers Edition*. 1965; rpt. New York: Norton, 1968. A reprint of the CEAA ed.

Bridgman, Richard, ed. *Leaves of Grass by Walt Whitman*. San Francisco: Chandler, 1968. A facsimile reprint of the first edition, 1855.

Miller, James E., Jr. *Complete Poetry and Selected Prose by Walt Whitman*. Boston: Houghton Mifflin, 1959. A popular classroom text in the Riverside series.

Biographies

Allen, Gay Wilson. *The Solitary Singer*. 1955; rev. New York: New York Univ. Press, 1967. The standard biography.

Asselineau, Roger. *The Evolution of Walt Whitman*. 2 vols. Cambridge: The Belknap Press of the Harvard Univ. Press, 1960-1962. Volume 1 is subtitled *The Creation of A Personality*.

Canby, Henry S. *Walt Whitman, An American: A Study in Biography*. Boston: Houghton Mifflin, 1943.

Letters and Journals

Bucke, Richard M., ed. *Wound Dresser: Letters Written to His Mother from the Hospitals in Washington during the Civil War*. New York: Bodley Press, 1949.

Kennedy, William Sloane, ed. *Walt Whitman's Diary in Canada*. Boston: Small, Maynard, 1904.

Miller, Edwin H., ed. *The Correspondence of Walt Whitman*, 3 vols. New York: New York Univ. Press. 1961-64.

Stovall, Floyd, ed. *Prose Works, 1892: Volume I, Specimen Days; Volume II, Collect and Other Prose*. New York: New York Univ. Press, 1962, 1963.

Bibliography

Current bibliography appears quarterly in the *Walt Whitman Review* and *American Literature*, annually in the June issue of *PMLA*, and in *American Literary Scholarship: An Annual, 1963*, ed. James Woodress, Durham: Duke Univ. Press, 1964- .

Allen, G. W. *Twenty-five Years of Walt Whitman Bibliography, 1918-1942*. Boston: Houghton Mifflin, 1943.

Allen, G. W. *Walt Whitman As Man, Poet and Legend: With a Checklist of Whitman Publications, 1945-1960*. Carbondale: Southern Illinois Press, 1961.

Leary, Lewis. *Articles on American Literature 1900-1950*. Durham: Duke Univ. Press, 1954. Pp. 303-16.

Spiller, Robert E., et al. *Literary History of the United States: Bibliography*, 3rd ed., rev.;

New York: Macmillan, 1963. Pp. 159-68, 203-207.

Thorp, Willard. "Walt Whitman," *Eight American Authors: A Review of Research and Criticism,* ed. Floyd Stovall. 1956; 3rd. ed. Durham: Duke Univ. Press, 1971.

Critical Studies

Allen, G. W. *Walt Whitman Handbook.* Chicago: Univ. of Chicago Press, 1946. An excellent introduction to Whitman studies.

Arvin, Newton. *Whitman.* New York: Macmillan, 1938. Strong political bias.

Asselineau, Roger. *The Evolution of Walt Whitman.* 2 vols. Cambridge: The Belknap Press of Harvard Univ. Press, 1960-1962. Vol. II is subtitled *The Creation of A Book.*

Chase, Richard. *Walt Whitman Reconsidered.* New York: William Sloane Associates, 1955.

Feidelson, Charles, Jr. *Symbolism and American Literature.* 1953; rpt. Chicago: Univ. of Chicago Press, 1959.

Green, Martin. *Re-Appraisals: Some Commonsense Readings in American Literature.* 1965; rpt. New York: Norton, 1967.

Hindus, Milton, ed. *Leaves of Grass One Hundred Years After.* Palo Alto: Stanford Univ. Press, 1955.

Jarrell, Randall. *Poetry and the Age.* New York: Vintage Books, 1953.

Lawrence, D. H. *Studies in Classic American Literature.* 1923; rpt. New York: Viking, 1964.

Lewis, R. W. B. *The American Adam: Innocence, Tragedy, and Tradition in the Nineteenth Century.* 1955; rpt. Chicago: Univ. of Chicago Press, 1958.

Lewis, R. W. B., ed. *The Presence of Walt Whitman: Selected Papers from the English Institute.* New York: Columbia Univ. Press, 1962.

Martz, Louis L. *The Poem of the Mind.* New York: Oxford Univ. Press, 1966.

Matthiessen, F. O. *American Renaissance.* New York: Oxford Univ. Press, 1941. A classic study.

Miller, Edwin H. *Walt Whitman's Poetry: A Psychological Journey.* Boston: Houghton Mifflin, 1968.

Miller, James E. *A Critical Guide to Leaves of Grass.* Chicago: Univ. of Chicago Press, 1957.

Miller, James E., Karl Shapiro, and Bernice Slote. *Start With the Sun: Studies in Cosmic Poetry.* Lincoln Univ. of Nebraska Press, 1960. The influence of Whitman on D. H. Lawrence, Hart Crane, and Dylan Thomas.

Pearce, Roy Harvey. *The Continuity of American Poetry.* Princeton: Princeton Univ. Press, 1961. Probably the best one-volume study of American poetry.

Pearce, Roy Harvey, ed. *Whitman: A Collection of Critical Essays.* Englewood Cliffs: Prentice-Hall, 1962. Reprints parts of the Matthiessen, Feidelson, Lawrence, and Lewis selections in this book.

Schyberg, Frederick. *Walt Whitman.* 1933; trans. Evie Allison Allen, New York: Columbia Univ. Press, 1951.

Spencer, Benjamin T. *The Quest for Nationality.* Syracuse: Syracuse Univ. Press, 1957.

Tanner, Tony. *The Reign of Wonder: Naivety and Reality in American Literature.* 1965; rpt. New York: Harper and Row, 1967.

Waskow, Howard J. *Whitman: Explorations in Form.* Chicago: Univ. of Chicago Press, 1966.

Weimer, David. *The City As Metaphor.* New York: Random House, 1966. Whitman was the first poet of the city.

Critical Articles

Adams, R. P. "Whitman's 'Lilacs' and the Tradition of Pastoral Elegy," *PMLA*, 72 (1957), 479-87.

Bradley, Sculley. "The Fundamental Metrical Principle in Whitman's Poetry," *American Literature*, 10 (1939), 437-59.

Chari, V. K. "Whitman and Indian Thought," *Western Humanities Review*, 13 (1959), 291-302.

Christ, Ronald. "Walt Whitman: Image and Credo," *American Quarterly*, 17 (1965), 92-103.

Eby, E. H. "Walt Whitman's Indirections," *Walt Whitman Review*, 12 (1966), 5-16.

Ghodes, Clarence L. "Whitman and Emerson," *Sewanee Review*, 37 (1929), 79-93.

Spitzer, Leo. "Explication de Texte Applied to Walt Whitman's 'Out of the Cradle Endlessly Rocking,' " *ELH*, 16 (1949), 229-49.

Strauch, Carl. "The Structure of Walt Whitman's 'Song of Myself,' " *English Journal* (College Edition), 27 (1938), 597-607.